Questions and Answers in Medical Ethics Core Cases

Emma Searle MBChB
Senior House Officer in Haematology
Salford Royal Hospitals
NHS Trust
Greater Manchester

Andrew Sewart MBChB
Foundation Year 1
Lancaster Royal Infirmary
Lancaster

Martin J Vernon MA FRCP (London)
Consultant Geriatrician
South Manchester University Hospitals NHS Trust
Manchester

Dedicated to your success

© 2006 PasTest Ltd

Egerton Court
Parkgate Estate
Knutsford
Cheshire, WA16 8DX

Telephone: 01565 752000

First edition 2006

ISBN: 1 904627 61 7
978 1 904627 61 6

A catalogue record for this book is available from the British Library.

The information contained within this book was obtained by the authors from reliable sources. However, while every effort has been made to ensure its accuracy, no responsibility for loss, damage or injury occasioned to any person acting or refraining from action as a result of information contained herein can be accepted by the publisher or the authors.

PasTest Revision Books and Intensive Courses

PasTest has been established in the field of postgraduate medical education since 1972, providing revision books and intensive study courses for doctors preparing for their professional examinations.

Books and courses are available for the following specialties:

MRCGP, MRCP Parts 1 and 2, MRCPCH Parts 1 and 2, MRCPsych, MRCS, MRCOG Parts 1 and 2, DRCOG, DCH, FRCA, PLAB Parts 1 and 2, Dental Students, Dentists and Dental Nurses.

For further details contact:

PasTest, Freepost, Knutsford, Cheshire WA16 7BR

Tel: 01565 752000   **Fax: 01565 650264**

www.pastest.co.uk   **enquires@pastest.co.uk**

Text prepared by Carnegie Book Production, Lancaster
Cover design: The Old Tin Dog Design Company

Printed and bound in the UK by Athenaeum Press

CONTENTS

FOREWORD

Practising doctors cannot avoid making clinical decisions which have ethical consequences. Health care is becoming ever more complex and expensive. Patients with access to seemingly unlimited online resources are increasingly aware of the treatment possibilities. Government- and media-driven expectations around choice, together with legally robust rights to life, privacy and freedom all conspire to make previously straightforward decisions fraught and open to challenge.

To newly qualified health professionals all this will seem daunting. Where does one begin to get answers? What approach can be taken? What are the pitfalls? Dealing with topics ranging from consent to confidentiality, organ donation to screening, advance directives to euthanasia, this book should be a starting point for any health professional faced with today's common ethical dilemmas.

The book has been designed to assist doctors and other health professionals with making difficult everyday choices. Using familiar clinical scenarios, the reader is challenged to consider the key ethical and legal issues which underlie their decisions. Structured answers and teaching notes allow the reader to self-assess their knowledge and build greater understanding. In such a small volume it is impossible to do full justice to the many and complex issues which underlie each topic area. Each chapter should be regarded as a starting point, and references (which are largely web-based) encourage the interested reader to direct their own learning thereafter.

Ethically robust decision making requires considerable expertise. However, armed with this volume, we hope that you will begin to develop your own understanding and views in ways which will assist you throughout your career.

Martin J Vernon
Consultant Physician and Geriatrician

INTRODUCTION

Medical ethics is an area that is playing an increasingly large part in medical exams, at both undergraduate and postgraduate levels. In this book we have tried to provide a clear guide to thinking around some of the commonly encountered ethical problems, using PBL-style (problem-based learning) scenarios, as faced by many students in their exams, and encountered on the wards.

We hope that even those who have considerably less interest in medical ethics than we have will find this short volume easy to digest, and through it increase their understanding of this important subject. Just like any other area of your practice, you must be able to justify the ethical decisions you make about your patients. We hope this is a starting place from which your ethical awareness might grow.

Emma Searle and Andy Sewart
2006

ACKNOWLEDGEMENTS

Illustrations created by Claire Searle, Medical Student, Leicester University.

GLOSSARY

A&E	Accident and Emergency
ANH	Artificial nutrition and hydration
BMA	British Medical Association
BP	Blood pressure
CMO	Chief Medical Officer
CPR	Cardiopulmonary resuscitation
CPS	Crown Prosecution Service
CVS	Chorionic villus sampling
DNR	Do not resuscitate
DPP	Director of Public Prosecutions
DVLA	Driver and Vehicle Licensing Agency
ESRF	End–stage renal failure
GMC	General Medical Council
HLA	Human leukocyte antigen
ITU	Intensive Therapy Unit
IV	Intravenous
MS	Multiple sclerosis
NG	Nasogastric
NHS	National Health Service
NT	Nuchal translucency
PEG	Percutaneous endoscopic gastrostomy
PVS	Persistent vegetative state
RCOG	Royal College of Obstetricians and Gynaecologists
REC	Research ethics committee
ULTRA	Unrelated Live Transplant Regulatory Authority

SCENARIO 1: ADVANCE DIRECTIVES

QUESTIONS

SCENARIO 1: ADVANCE DIRECTIVES

Tom, a lifelong smoker with end-stage respiratory disease, is brought into A&E with extreme dyspnoea. From his past medical history he is considered at high risk of cardiopulmonary arrest. He informs you as the admitting doctor that he has made an advance directive.

Give 2 forms which his advance directive may take.   **2 marks**

1.

2.

Tom hands you his advance directive, which states that should he arrest he does not want to be resuscitated.

List 4 of your responsibilities regarding Tom's advance directive.   **4 marks**

1.

2.

3.

4.

Name 2 wishes that advance directives cannot request.   **4 marks**

1.
_____

2.
_____

Give 2 advantages and 2 disadvantages of an advance
directive.   **4 marks**

Advantages:

1.
_____

2.
_____

Disadvantages:

1.
_____

2.
_____

*Tom's wife is informed of the DNR order made on the
basis of his valid advance directive. She is unhappy with
this treatment decision and asks you to perform CPR if
her husband arrests.*

Name 2 of his human rights that would be broken if CPR were
performed (with a short explanation).   **4 marks**

1.
_____

2.
_____

4

Give 2 other situations when CPR should not be attempted.   *1 mark*

1.

2.

In the absence of an advance directive, who *typically* has the final say on whether an incapacitated patient should undergo CPR?   *1 mark*

1.

Total: *20 marks*

SCENARIO 2:
CONSENT IN MINORS

QUESTIONS

SCENARIO 2: CONSENT IN MINORS

Andy, a 14-year-old schoolboy, is involved in a road traffic accident. On arrival at A&E he is alert, has a closed fracture of his humerus, and is complaining of abdominal pain. His BP is noted to be dropping and an abdominal scan is suggestive of a ruptured spleen. You advise him that he will need a blood transfusion and an emergency operation.

At what age is a minor presumed to be competent to give consent for treatment? Which statute specifies this in England and Wales? **2 marks**

1.

2.

List one similarity and one difference between consent under this statute and consent in adults? **2 marks**

Similarity:
1.

Difference:
1.

9

You assess Andy to determine whether he is competent to consent to the blood transfusion and emergency operation.

In Andy's case which common law test should be used to determine if he is competent to give consent to treatment?   *1 mark*

1.

Explain the 2 factors considered in this test.   *2 marks*

1.

2.

You deem Andy to be competent and he consents to the proposed treatment.

Give 4 examples of people/agencies with parental responsibility who can consent to treatment on behalf of a child who is not competent.   *4 marks*

1.

2.

3.

4.

As Andy is being prepared for surgery his parents arrive and are informed of events. They instruct you that they do not want Andy to receive blood products on religious grounds, refusing to consent to the blood transfusion.

Give 2 examples of when parental consent may not be valid. **2 marks**

1.

2.

Under pressure from his parents, Andy is dissuaded from consenting to the blood transfusion.

List 2 examples of people/agencies who might overrule refusal of treatment by a competent minor. **2 marks**

1.

2.

List 2 examples of situations in which doctors may proceed with emergency treatment considered to be in the child's best interests without consent. **2 marks**

1.

2.

Consent in Minors

Do you have a legal responsibility to inform Andy's parents if he decides to have the blood transfusion against their wishes?   *1 mark*

1.

_____

Total: *18 marks*

ANSWERS
PAGES 61–72

SCENARIO 3: EUTHANASIA AND ASSISTED DYING

QUESTIONS

SCENARIO 3: EUTHANASIA AND ASSISTED DYING

Jane is a 45-year-old woman who 10 years previously had been diagnosed with multiple sclerosis (MS). She has suffered a turbulent course of her illness, and after several relapses and remissions has acquired a high level of disability. Her use of an electric wheelchair is one way in which she indicates her clear wish to remain independent. You are Jane's GP. Today she visits with her husband, Rob, to discuss a pressing issue. During her illness you have come to know Jane well, and now she asks you, as her family doctor, to advise her regarding 'ending it all' when she feels her life is no longer worth living.

What is euthanasia?   *1 mark*

1.

Jane states that if you are not prepared to actively end her life then she wants your word that she will not receive treatment for any future life-threatening illness she might develop in addition to her MS.

Briefly distinguish between the terms 'active euthanasia' and 'passive euthanasia'. *2 marks*

1. Active euthanasia:

2. Passive euthanasia:

Is active euthanasia permissible under UK law? *1 mark*

1.

Outline 4 arguments in favour of euthanasia. *4 marks*

1.

2.

3.

4.

Outline 4 arguments against euthanasia. *4 marks*

1.

2.

3.

4.

*Jane says that she has been considering travelling to
Switzerland where she has read on the Internet that they
allow 'physician-assisted suicide'.*

What is meant by the term 'physician-assisted suicide'?   *1 mark*

1.

List 3 arguments in favour of physician-assisted suicide over active
euthanasia.   *3 marks*

1.

2.

3.

*Jane asks if it is true that doctors sometimes 'give extra
morphine to help speed things up at the end'.*

Briefly explain the doctrine of double effect and how this
might relate to the administration of morphine during the dying
phase.   *2 marks*

1.

2.

Total: *18 marks*

**ANSWERS
PAGES 73–90**

17

SCENARIO 4: ANTENATAL SCREENING AND ABORTION

QUESTIONS

SCENARIO 4: ANTENATAL SCREENING AND ABORTION

Hannah, a 38-year-solicitor, attends her local obstetric outpatients for her antenatal care. Because of her age she is offered a screening test for Down's syndrome.

What information should you give Hannah about the screening test?   ***4 marks***

1.

2.

3.

4.

Give 3 advantages and 3 disadvantages of antenatal screening.   ***6 marks***

Advantages:

1.

2.

3.

Disadvantages:

1.

2.

3.

The screening test is positive and amniocentesis confirms that her baby has Down's syndrome. She is distraught and requests an abortion.

Outline the legal frameworks that govern abortion in the UK. *2 marks*

1.

2.

Up to what gestational age could Hannah's pregnancy be legally terminated due to Down's syndrome? *1 mark*

1.

List 3 legal criteria for abortion other than fetal abnormality. *3 marks*

1.

2.

3.

What legal right does Hannah's partner have in her decision to terminate the pregnancy? **1 mark**

1.
_____

What are the wider implications for society of abortion on request? **3 marks**

1.
_____

2.
_____

3.
_____

Total: **20 marks**

Antenatal Screening

ANSWERS PAGES 91–104

23

SCENARIO 5: WITHHOLDING AND WITHDRAWING TREATMENT

QUESTIONS

SCENARIO 5: WITHHOLDING AND WITHDRAWING TREATMENT

Maeve is an 80-year-old woman admitted to A&E from a nursing home and is barely conscious on arrival. She has a past medical history of Alzheimer's disease, diabetes, hypertension, rheumatoid arthritis, chronic renal failure and a previous stroke. On this occasion she is found to be suffering from pneumonia and dehydration, and tests show evidence of a recent myocardial infarction (MI). Her carer tells you that Maeve has little quality of life; she is in constant pain, is unable to interact meaningfully with others, is frequently very distressed and eats and drinks little.

What is meant by the term 'active treatment'? *1 mark*

1.

List 4 arguments for and 4 arguments against withdrawal of active treatment in this situation. **8 marks**

For:

1.

2.

3.

4.

Against:

1.

2.

3.

4.

Maeve's daughter arrives. She feels that her mother would not have wanted to be treated for this illness.

Describe 2 other ways in which you might ascertain a patient's wishes with regard to withholding/withdrawing treatment. **2 marks**

1.

2.

List 2 steps that may be taken in the event that relatives and doctors strongly disagree about the decision to withhold/withdraw active treatment from a patient who lacks capacity. **2 marks**

1.

2.

Can a competent patient insist that life-prolonging treatment be provided? **1 mark**

1.

Maeve is admitted to the medical assessment unit where she is reviewed by the on-call consultant who agrees with the family's wish that Maeve should not be given antibiotics.

List 4 responsibilities you have following the decision to withhold treatment. **4 marks**

1.

2.

3.

4.

Withholding Treatment

Maeve's condition declines rapidly over the next few hours and she is now clearly dying. It becomes difficult to insert an intravenous drip to maintain hydration.

Can the medical team legally withdraw artificial hydration?   *1 mark*

1.

Total: *19 marks*

ANSWERS
PAGES 105–118

SCENARIO 6: CONSENT IN ADULTS

QUESTIONS

SCENARIO 6: CONSENT IN ADULTS

Catherine is an 83-year-old woman who was admitted from home following a collapse. She has been very fit and well her whole life, except that over the last few months she has been suffering increasingly with chest pain and breathlessness. After several tests it is discovered that she has severe aortic stenosis (a serious problem with one of the valves in her heart). Despite optimal medical treatment she continues to remain symptomatic and a decision must be made about surgical management. She has no other significant medical history but does report being 'a little forgetful at times'.

Outline 3 ethical arguments for obtaining valid consent for treatment in adults. **3 marks**

1.

2.

3.

Which 3 conditions must be met in order for consent to be legally valid? *3 marks*

1.

2.

3.

Catherine tells you that she is keen to pursue surgery but she would like to know a few more facts, in particular if it is possible that she might die during the operation.

Do you have to inform Catherine about all the possible risks of her surgery? *1 mark*

1.

List 3 legally acceptable forms of consent to medical treatment. *3 marks*

1.

2.

3.

Catherine's family confront you, furious that you have allowed Catherine to agree to surgery 'at her age'.

Give 3 conditions that must be met for an adult to be deemed to have capacity to consent to medical treatment. **3 marks**

1.

2.

3.

List 2 situations in which consent to treatment is not legally required in adults. **2 marks**

1.

2.

List 4 factors which, legally or ethically, you should take into consideration when deciding to treat a patient who lacks capacity for decision making. **4 marks**

1.

2.

3.

4.

Consent in Adults

35

Can Catherine's family overrule her legally valid agreement to treatment?   *1 mark*

1.

___

Total: **20 marks**

ANSWERS
PAGES 119–136

SCENARIO 7: ORGAN DONATION

QUESTIONS

# SCENARIO 7: ORGAN DONATION

Dave is a 25-year-old engineer who was diagnosed with polycystic kidney disease. He progressed to end-stage renal failure (ESRF), and received a transplant. However, he did not attend the clinic or take his anti-rejection drugs regularly and his transplant failed. Suniti is a 32-year-old mother of three children, who also has ESRF as the result of diabetes. They are both receiving dialysis three times a week at their local hospital, and are on the transplant list.

List 4 criteria that may be used to prioritise patients waiting for transplant.   **4 marks**

1.

2.

3.

4.

Organ donation

Give 2 arguments for and 2 arguments against prioritisation on the basis of self-inflicted illness. **4 marks**

For:

1.

2.

Against:

1.

2.

> *Dave receives his second organ transplant, but Suniti is still waiting. She has heard it is more difficult for people of Asian origin to find a compatible donor.*

What are the disadvantages of the current 'organ donation' system? **4 marks**

1.

2.

3.

4.

Organ donation

What are the advantages of presumed consent?   *4 marks*

1.

2.

3.

4.

You hear that Suniti has been talking to other patients on the dialysis unit and that her husband is thinking of taking her to India to 'buy her a new kidney'.

Give 2 arguments for and 2 arguments against allowing kidney sales.   *4 marks*

For:
1.

2.

Against:
1.

2.

Total: *20 marks*

SCENARIO 8: CONFIDENTIALITY

QUESTIONS

SCENARIO 8:
CONFIDENTIALITY

During his teenage years Stephen contracted hepatitis C while experimenting with intravenous drugs. He hasn't touched drugs for over 10 years now and is happily married, with a responsible job. At one of his regular outpatient appointments his gastroenterologist offers him the chance to participate in a clinical trial to help clear his virus.

In seeking Stephen's consent, what information about the trial needs to be provided?   **5 marks**

1.

2.

3.

4.

5.

Stephen is keen to participate in the trial but is concerned that as a result his employers may discover he is hepatitis C positive.

Why is confidentiality important?   *2 marks*

1.

2.

How do you protect patient confidentiality?   *4 marks*

1.

2.

3.

4.

Under what situations may breach of patient confidence be
justifiable?   *5 marks*

1.

2.

3.

4.

5.

*Stephen is satisfied by your reassurances of
confidentiality and commences on the trial the following
week.*

What are your responsibilities as a researcher?   *4 marks*

1.

2.

3.

4.

Total: *20 marks*

Confidentiality

SCENARIO 1: ADVANCE DIRECTIVES

ANSWERS

SCENARIO 1: ADVANCE DIRECTIVES

Tom, a lifelong smoker with end-stage respiratory disease, is brought into A&E with extreme dyspnoea. From his past medical history he is considered at high risk of cardiopulmonary arrest. He informs you as the admitting doctor that he has made an advance directive.

Q Give 2 forms which his advance directive may take.   ***2 marks***

1. Written document.

2. Witnessed oral statement (which might also have been documented in writing in the patient's file).

❶ An advance directive is a statement, oral or written, in which a competent, appropriately informed adult voluntarily gives instructions on how they should be treated clinically if they should become incompetent.

❶ The instructions contained in an advance directive may be in one of several forms:

a. *Treatment refusal or acceptance:* a clear instruction on which medical treatments (eg transfusion) they would refuse/accept in a range of circumstances, eg elective surgical procedures. **Considered legally binding.**

b. *Refusal of life-sustaining treatment:* a statement refusing life-sustaining treatment, eg artificial nutrition and hydration, under clearly defined conditions such as severe acquired brain injury. **Considered legally binding.**

QUESTIONS
PAGES 1–6

c. *Treatment preferences:* a statement reflecting a patient's preferences, eg to be treated at home. **Used to guide health professionals, though it may not be legally binding if it conflicts with their clinical judgement.**

d. *Appointment of proxy:* a statement naming another person who should be consulted when decisions are made (the views expressed by the named person should reflect the views of the patient). **Legally binding in Scotland (The Adults with Incapacity [Scotland] Act 2000 allows for a proxy decision-maker to refuse treatment on behalf of an incapacitated person over the age of 16 years).** In England and Wales similar arrangements will apply under the terms of the Mental Capacity Act 2005, which becomes effective in 2007. See www.opsi.gov.uk/acts (Last accessed April 2006) and www.dca.gov.uk (Last accessed April 2006) for code of practice.

Tom hands you his advance directive which states that should he arrest he does not want to be resuscitated.

Q List 4 of your responsibilities regarding Tom's advance directive. *4 marks*

1. **Ensure you are familiar with the contents of the advance directive.**

2. **Ensure the contents of Tom's advance directive still represent his present views.**

3. **Make sure a copy is placed on all the relevant files.**

4. **Make sure all staff involved in Tom's care are aware of it.**

5. **Recognise the validity of the advance statement (do not act against the patient's wishes).**

🛈 Late discovery of an advance directive is not sufficient grounds for ignoring it. However, treatment already administered in good faith contrary to a discovered valid advance directive is unlikely to be considered wrongful. In addition, in the event of an emergency (or doubts about a directive's validity), treatment should not be delayed while awaiting clarification of the directive.

Q Name 2 wishes that advance directives cannot request. **4 marks**

Advance directives cannot:

1. **Require specific treatments.**

2. **Require doctors to break the law, eg euthanasia.**

3. **Refuse treatment where its omission would pose a risk to others, eg basic hygiene.**

4. **Refuse basic care: treatments that solely provide comfort to the patient, eg pain relief, warmth.**

🛈 ANH, is *not* considered basic care but medical treatment.

🛈 Whether a patient could demand ANH in an advance directive was tested in the case of *Burke* v *GMC*. See the Teaching notes for Scenario 5, Withholding and withdrawing treatment for more detail on this case.

Q Give 2 advantages and 2 disadvantages of an advance directive. **4 marks**

Advantages:

1. **Allows the patient to continue to exercise prior autonomy even when incapacitated.**

2. **Helps guide doctors' treatment decisions in difficult cases.**

3. **Assists in removing the anxiety relatives may feel when deciding on future treatment.**

Disadvantages:

1. **The patient may feel pressured into making a certain decision, eg if worrying about becoming a burden.**

2. **Difficult to keep up to date: it is impossible to predict how the disease may progress and new treatments might develop.**

3. **The healthy do not choose in the same way as the sick – it is impossible to predict how you might feel.**

4. **In all cases a contemporaneous statement made by a competent patient (even if only an oral statement) overrides an earlier advance statement.**

5. **The advance directive may be misinterpreted.**

6. **The advance directive may not be specific to the patient's condition under consideration.**

7. **Often difficult to validate and easy to contest, especially if oral.**

8. **Often difficult to communicate to all relevant health professionals at the relevant time.**

9. **Advance directives are poorly understood and have yet to be widely accepted and so may simply be ignored.**

🛈 If the clinical situation is not identical to the one described in the advance directive, though no longer legally binding, doctors should act in the general spirit of the statement.

Tom's wife is informed of the DNR order made on the basis of his valid advance directive. She is unhappy with this treatment decision and asks you to perform CPR if her husband arrests.

Q Name 2 of his human rights that would be broken if CPR were performed (with a short explanation). *4 marks*

1. **Article 3: prohibition of torture, inhumane or degrading treatment.** CPR could be considered degrading in that it does not allow a peaceful death.

2. **Article 8: respect for privacy and family life.** Tom has a right to be involved in his medical decisions, including the right to refuse CPR.

3. **Article 9: freedom of thought, conscience and religion:** Tom has the right of freedom to act upon his beliefs, in this case to refuse CPR.

🔵 Details of how the Human Rights Act impacts on medical practice is summarised in the Teaching notes for this scenario.

Q Give 2 other situations when CPR should not be attempted. *1 mark*

1. **Where attempting CPR is clearly futile.**

2. **Where there is no benefit in restarting the patient's heart and breathing, eg where successful CPR only offers brief extension of life as co-morbidity means that death is imminent.**

3. **Where the expected benefit is outweighed by the burdens: this is the most difficult to assess as it requires balancing of the benefits of prolonging life against the burdens, eg side-effects of traumatic CPR, prolonged hypoxia.**

🔵 CPR should also not be performed in the presence of a valid advance directive refusing CPR or if, following discussions, a mentally competent patient makes an informed decision not to undergo CPR.

🔵 However, in any patient assessed as DNR it needs to be made clear to both the patient (where competent) and the family that this does not mean that other treatments will be withheld, but that every effort will be made to avoid cardiopulmonary arrest. Every hospital should have a local policy on CPR.

Q In the absence of an advance directive, who **typically** has the final say on whether an incapacitated patient should undergo CPR? *1 mark*

1. **The doctor who has overall responsibility for the patient's care (usually the consultant).**

ⓘ If the patient is unable to give consent, the doctor with overall responsibility for care has a duty to determine the patient's best interests in consultation with all relevant members of the clinical team and those with a legitimate interest in the patient's wellbeing (such as family members). The family do not have the final say on whether CPR should be attempted. However, the responsible doctor should seek advice from the patient's family in order to reflect the patient's preferences (though not their own preferences).

ⓘ However, it should be noted that if there is significant disagreement on whether to provide CPR (or any other form of medical treatment), which cannot be resolved locally through informal or independent review, the doctor should take legal advice about seeking a ruling from the Court. This requirement now has legal recognition: see Scenario 6, Consent in adults, and the section on *Glass v the United Kingdom*, in the Teaching notes for Scenario 3, Euthanasia and assisted dying.

Total: **20** *marks*

You may also wish to read the following British Medical Association (BMA) paper (available at www.bma.org.uk): *Advance statements about medical treatments – code of practice.*

SCENARIO 1: ADVANCE DIRECTIVES

TEACHING NOTES

The impact of the Human Rights Act on medical practice

The Human Rights Act 1998 (which actually came into force in 2000) incorporates into UK law the European Convention on Human Rights.

This means that:

1. If someone believes that their human rights have been violated they can take this to the UK courts rather than to the European Court in Strasbourg.

2. Public authorities, eg the NHS, are required to act in a way that is compatible with the Convention on Human Rights.

There are a number of rights set out in the Human Rights Act (termed 'articles') including:

1. Right to life (article 2)

2. Prohibition of torture, inhumane or degrading treatment (article 3)

3. Right to liberty and security (article 5)

4. Right to a fair trial (article 6)

5. Respect for privacy and family life (article 8)

6. Freedom of thought, conscience and religion (article 9)

7. Right to marry and have a family (article 12)

8. Prohibition of discrimination (article 14)

These rights are divided into three types:

1. **Absolute rights**, ie no alternative (derogation) is allowed, eg prohibition of torture.

2. **Limited rights**, ie limitations are clearly stated in the Act itself, eg right to life (except when sentenced to death under law).

3. **Qualified rights**, ie where alternatives are permitted but must be legal and **proportionate**, eg breaking someone's right to privacy, such as reporting an unfit doctor to the GMC.

The term **proportionate** means that the extent of interference in someone's human rights must be justifiable. This simply involves balancing competing interests (which is not new in ethics). For example, if you decide to breach confidentiality between you and a patient (article 8) you must be able to justify your reasons for doing so: preventing a serious crime would be considered proportionate, whereas gossiping with friends would not be considered proportionate.

The practical impact of article 2 on medical practice is discussed below:

Article 2: right to life

The right to life does not mean that a doctor must always try to prolong life at all costs; however, it could be argued that withholding or withdrawing treatment could breach article 2. However, as long as withholding/withdrawing treatment is in the patient's best interests it is justified; furthermore, futile treatment could breach article 3, ie prohibition of inhumane or degrading treatment.

Patients can waive their right to life by making an informed refusal of life-prolonging treatment.

Patients could claim that a doctor's failure to warn them about a known risk to their life, eg an HIV-positive partner, contravenes their right to life; it is possible that the patient's right to life (article 2) conflicts with the sexual partner's right to privacy (article 8).

Treatment that could prolong life is sometimes withheld due to lack of money, eg an expensive new drug for cancer treatment. Patients who could benefit from such a drug could argue that its restriction contravenes their right to life. However, they would need to demonstrate that failing to provide treatment would inevitably lead to death and that providing treatment would prevent death.

When allocating resources, the NHS has to show that it has considered the patient's human rights, namely:

1. The right to life of the patients who would receive the new drug.

2. The right to life of patients who would not receive their existing treatments if the resources were now spent on this new drug.

3. Any decision must be non-discriminatory (article 14).

You may also wish to read the following BMA paper available at www.bma.org.uk in the ethics section: *The impact of the Human Rights Act 1998 on medical decision making.*

SCENARIO 2:
CONSENT IN MINORS

ANSWERS

SCENARIO 2: CONSENT IN MINORS

Andy, a 14-year-old schoolboy, is involved in a road traffic accident. On arrival at A&E he is alert, has a closed fracture of his humerus, and is complaining of abdominal pain. His BP is noted to be dropping and an abdominal scan is suggestive of a ruptured spleen. You advise him that he will need a blood transfusion and an emergency operation.

Q At what age is a minor presumed to be competent to give consent for treatment? Which statute specifies this in England and Wales?

2 marks

1. **Patients aged 16 and over are presumed competent to give consent for treatment.**

2. **Family Law Reform Act 1969.**

🔵 The Family Law Reform Act places the 16- to 18-year-old in the same position as an adult, ie they are presumed competent to make decisions about surgical, medical or dental treatment plus ancillary and diagnostic procedures such as administration of a general anaesthetic. Procedures that are not surgical, medical or dental treatment, such as organ or blood donation, are not included because they are not treatment or diagnostic interventions.

🔵 In relation to other decisions 16- to 18-year-olds are dealt with as per the rules for younger children, ie the Gillick test of competence applies (see below).

QUESTIONS
PAGES 7–12

🛈 This is well covered in Kennedy I. Grubb A. *Medical Law*. 3rd ed. London: Butterworths, 2000, p. 645, should you wish to read more.

Q List one similarity and one difference between consent under this statute and consent in adults?   *2 marks*

Similarity:

1. **As for adults (ie 18 years or over), consent will only be valid if the minor (<18 years) has the capacity to consent to the particular treatment.**

Difference:

1. **Unlike adults, the *refusal* of a competent person aged 16–17 years may in certain circumstances be overridden by either a person with parental responsibility or a court (see below).**

2. **Unlike adults, valid consent cannot be given for non-therapeutic interventions.**

You assess Andy to determine whether he is competent to consent to the blood transfusion and emergency operation.

Q In Andy's case, which common law test should be used to determine if he is competent to give consent to treatment? *1 mark*

1. **The Gillick (or Fraser) principle.**

🛈 The case of *Gillick v West Norfolk and Wisbech Area Health Authority* [1986] AC 112 established this principle, which concerns when valid consent may be obtained in those aged under 16 years. This involves determining whether the child is capable of understanding what is proposed (see next answer).

Q Explain the 2 factors considered in this test.   *2 marks*

1. **The minor must have sufficient intelligence and understanding to understand the illness.**

2. **The minor must have sufficient intelligence and understanding to understand the proposed treatment (and its side-effects and complications).**

🟦 A child is considered Gillick competent if they are capable of understanding what is involved, which in turn depends on the child's maturity and developmental state. 'What is involved' entails 'the nature, purpose and likely consequences' of undergoing the procedure, which might include the long-term consequences and risks.

🟦 Each different treatment in each different child must be considered on a case-by-case basis, as the levels of understanding and intelligence required will vary greatly between treatments.

You deem Andy to be competent and he consents to the proposed treatment.

Q Give 4 examples of people/agencies with parental responsibility who can consent to treatment on behalf of a child who is not competent.   *4 marks*

1. **The child's mother.**

2. **The child's father (see note overleaf).**

3. **A person in whose favour the court has made a residence order concerning the child.**

4. **A local authority designated in a care order in respect of the child.**

Consent in Minors

5. **A local authority or other authorised person who holds an emergency protection order in respect of the child.**

● The Children Act 1989 sets out persons who may have parental responsibility. Only these people can give valid consent.

● Traditionally, fathers were only considered to have parental responsibility if either married to the mother at the time of conception, birth or subsequently, or if the father has acquired parental responsibility via a court order or parental responsibility agreement. However, the law changed in Northern Ireland in 2002 and in England and Wales in 2004 to give unmarried fathers parental responsibility if they registered (or re-registered) the birth together with the mother, so avoiding the need in most cases to get court declaration.

● Under this Act, a person who has parental responsibility 'may arrange for some or all of it to be met by one or more persons acting on his behalf' (eg a childminder). This is usually in a written form. Those without parental responsibility but who care for the child may 'do what is reasonable in all the circumstances for the purpose of safeguarding or promoting the child's welfare'. While a bit vague, it does for example allow teachers to consent to the treatment of minor injuries for children in their care.

As Andy is being prepared for surgery his parents arrive and are informed of events. They instruct you that they do not want Andy to receive blood products on religious grounds, refusing to consent to the blood transfusion.

Q Give 2 examples of when parental consent may not be valid.   *2 marks*

1. **Where those with parental responsibility disagree with each other as to whether non-therapeutic procedures are in the child's best interests.**

2. Where the person with parental responsibility does not have capacity.

3. Where a child is a ward of court.

🟦 The courts have stated that a 'small group of important decisions' should not be taken where different individuals with parental responsibility disagree as to whether consent should be given. An example would be non-therapeutic male circumcision. In this case the matter should be referred to court.

🟦 If the mother of a child is under 16 years, she can only give valid consent if she is deemed to be Gillick competent herself.

🟦 If the child is a ward of court, no important step can be taken in the life of the child without prior consent from the court.

Under pressure from his parents, Andy is dissuaded from consenting to the blood transfusion.

Q List 2 examples of people/agencies who might overrule refusal of treatment by a competent minor. **2 marks**

1. A person with parental responsibility for the child.

2. The courts.

🟦 When a minor considered to be competent (under either the Family Law Reform Act or according to the Gillick principle) refuses consent for a treatment, this may be overruled by the courts or by any one person with parental responsibility.

🟦 This is a very difficult area, and it has previously been said that this should only apply in circumstances in which 'grave and irreversible mental or physical harm' would result from the intervention being refused and it must be in the child's best interests.

Consent in Minors

Q List 2 examples of situations in which doctors may proceed with emergency treatment considered to be in the child's best interests without consent. *2 marks*

1. **When a person with parental responsibility (or the court) cannot be consulted.**

2. **When those with parental responsibility refuse consent despite the need for emergency treatment that is considered to be in the best interests of the child.**

ℹ The courts have stated that it is permitted for doctors to act in the best interests of the child to preserve life or prevent serious damage to health in situations such as these.

Q Do you have a legal responsibility to inform Andy's parents if he decides to have the blood transfusion against their wishes? *1 mark*

1. **No.**

ℹ Children deemed able to give valid consent for treatment are entitled to the same degree of confidentiality with regard to that decision as an adult. However, it is considered good practice to encourage the child to discuss such decisions with their parents, unless you believe that this might cause harm to the child.

Total: *18 marks*

SCENARIO 2: CONSENT IN MINORS

TEACHING NOTES

Minors are defined in law as any person under the age of 18 years. It is important to get to grips with how to gain valid consent for interventions involving minors; the examiners just love questions in this area! A straightforward way to start is divide the problem into two areas: consent in those under 16 years and in those over this age.

Children over 16

Children aged 16 or 17 may give consent for treatment in the same way as adults, also meaning they must have capacity to give consent in the same way as adults (covered in Scenario 6, Consent in adults). This is provided for in England and Wales under the Family Law Reform Act 1969. The Act provides that:

> '... the consent of a minor who has attained the age of 16 years to any surgical, medical or dental treatment which, in the absence of consent, would constitute a trespass to his person, shall be as effective as it would be if he were of full age; and where a minor has by virtue of this section given an effective consent to any treatment it shall not be necessary to obtain any consent for it from his parent or guardian. In this section, surgical, medical or dental treatment includes any procedure undertaken for the purposes of diagnosis, and this section applies to any procedure (including, in particular, the administration of an anaesthetic) which is ancillary to any treatment as it applies to that treatment. Nothing in this section shall be construed as making ineffective any consent which would have been effective if this section had not been enacted.'

All far too much to remember! But, put simply, it means that minors aged 16 years or older can give consent to their own treatment and any diagnostic tests necessary for that treatment. A consent form does not also need to be signed or countersigned by a parent/guardian. They cannot, under this Act, give consent for procedures that do not directly benefit their health, eg research, but may well be able to under the Gillick rules as explained below.

Children under the age of 16

Under common law, children <16 years may under certain circumstances give consent following the case of *Gillick* v *West Norfolk and Wisbech Area Health Authority* [1986] AC 112. In this case Mrs Gillick challenged the legality of Department of Health advice to doctors that they could prescribe contraception to girls under 16 without the knowledge or consent of their parents. This eventually led to the House of Lords providing guidance on consent in children. This has been incorporated into Department of Heath Guidelines published in 2001, the key points of which are summarised below[1]:

[1]Department of Health. *Reference guide to consent for examination or treatment.* Crown Copyright, 2001

1. Children who have sufficient understanding and intelligence to enable them to understand fully what is involved in the proposed treatment, research or tissue donation have the capacity to give consent for it.

2. Different interventions will require different levels of understanding, meaning that a child under 16 may have capacity to consent to some interventions but not others.

3. It should not be assumed that a child with a learning difficulty does not have the capacity to give consent.

4. In a case where a child appears competent at one time, but not at others (eg due to their mental state) careful consideration should be given to whether the child is truly **Gillick** competent at any time.

5. Consent from a Gillick-competent child will be valid and additional consent by a person with parental responsibility is not required.

6. In a situation with ongoing implications (such as the long-term use of contraception) the child should be encouraged to inform their parents. This is unless it is clearly not in the child's best interests to do so, eg if you believe this would result in harm to the child.

 You may also wish to read the Department of Health's *Reference guide to consent for examination or treatment,* available on their website www.dh.gov.uk (Last accessed April 2006) in the policy and guidance section.

SCENARIO 3: EUTHANASIA AND ASSISTED DYING

ANSWERS

SCENARIO 3: EUTHANASIA AND ASSISTED DYING

Jane is a 45-year-old woman who 10 years previously had been diagnosed with multiple sclerosis (MS). She has suffered a turbulent course of her illness, and after several relapses and remissions has acquired a high level of disability. Her use of an electric wheelchair is one way in which she indicates her clear wish to remain independent. You are Jane's GP. Today she visits with her husband, Rob, to discuss a pressing issue. During her illness you have come to know Jane well, and now she asks you, as her family doctor, to advise her regarding 'ending it all' when she feels her life is no longer worth living.

Q What is euthanasia? *1 mark*

1. EXAMPLE ANSWER

Euthanasia is the action of directly causing the quick and painless death of a person, or omitting to prevent it when intervention was within the agent's powers. It is usually understood that euthanasia is performed only with the intention of relieving suffering and where death is perceived as the greater good or lesser evil for the patient.

Euthanasia, active/passive. In: Blackburn S. *The Oxford dictionary of philosophy*. Oxford: Oxford University Press, 1996 (*Oxford Reference Online*)

QUESTIONS
PAGES 13–18

🛈 Definitions of euthanasia vary, but there are certain key points that should be included in your answer:

a. It is deliberate.

b. It is done in the interests of the person concerned because death for that individual achieves a better outcome than continued life.

c. It is a 'good' death – painless/dignified.

🛈 The term 'euthanasia' is usually only applied in the context of people with a terminal illness such as advanced cancer, or progressive neurological disease. However, there are other clinical scenarios which are sometimes used to argue for the legalisation of euthanasia or physician-assisted suicide. Examples are severe and irreversible disability, intractable mental anguish or advanced age-related morbidity.

Jane states that if you are not prepared to actively end her life then she wants your word that she will not receive treatment for any future life-threatening illness she might develop in addition to her MS.

Q Briefly distinguish between the terms 'active euthanasia' and 'passive euthanasia'. **2 marks**

1. **Active euthanasia refers to an action that directly brings about the end to a patient's life, for example the administration of a lethal dose of a drug with the intention of killing that patient.**

2. **Passive euthanasia describes a situation in which a patient is allowed to die when an action that would keep them alive is deliberately not taken, eg antibiotics not given for an infection.**

❶ For each of these there is a further subdivision into voluntary, involuntary and non-voluntary:

a. **Voluntary euthanasia** concerns a circumstance in which euthanasia is performed at the request of the patient, eg they are provided with the means to end their own life, or it is ended with their consent.

b. **Involuntary euthanasia** is when euthanasia is employed without the consent of the patient concerned where valid consent could have been obtained. This might be expressly against their instruction, or without their knowledge and agreement.

c. **Non-voluntary euthanasia** applies where euthanasia is conducted without the consent of the patient concerned, where it is not possible to obtain valid consent, because of coma, dementia, etc.

Q Is active euthanasia permissible under UK law?   *1 mark*

1. No.

❶ In general, active forms of ending life are unlawful. It is unlawful to kill a person and is considered murder or manslaughter. In evidence submitted to the Assisted Dying for the Terminally Ill Bill in 2004 www.publications.parliament.uk the Attorney General stated, 'Deliberately taking the life of another person, whether that person is dying or not, constitutes the crime of murder. Accordingly, any doctor who practises mercy killing can be charged with murder if the facts can be clearly established.'

Full text of the Assisted Dying for the Terminally Ill Bill see www.publications.parliament.uk

🔵 However, this may not be the case for passive forms of euthanasia. The Tony Bland case (*Airedale NHS Trust* v *Bland* [1993] AC 789 (HL)) is acknowledged by many as permitting passive non-voluntary euthanasia under English law. Here the discontinuation of NG-tube feeding in a patient in a permanent vegetative state was considered lawful on the basis that continued feeding no longer served his best interests. Further information on this can be found in Scenario 5, Withholding and withdrawing treatment.

Q Outline 4 arguments in favour of euthanasia.　　　　*4 marks*

1. **Relief of intolerable suffering (non-maleficence).**

2. **Promotion of wellbeing and dignity (beneficence).**

3. **Respect for autonomy (patient choice).**

4. **Distributive justice (see notes below).**

🔵 There are certainly other arguments that might be included, eg allowing a patient to decide not to become reliant (a burden?) on their relatives, but the above are the key concepts.

🔵 It is also argued that it would be better to provide a legal framework for euthanasia (thus allowing for open control) than allowing what some fear is the current status quo with individual physicians already taking active steps to end life in exceptional circumstances. But this is more an argument for legalisation than for euthanasia itself.

Q Outline 4 arguments against euthanasia.　　　　*4 marks*

1. **Sanctity of life – might include religious and moral arguments.**

2. **The thin-end-of-the-wedge, or slippery-slope argument.**

3. **Regulatory frameworks are difficult to police.**

4. **Killing is a fundamental wrong for which there is no justification.**

5. **Loss of trust between patients, professionals and society in general.**

6. **Societys needs to protect its most vulnerable members (the elderly, those with disability, those lacking mental capacity).**

7. **Palliation provides a credible alternative.**

🛈 Again, there are other valid arguments relating to those above. Along with the concerns as to a robust regulatory framework are other practical considerations, eg the psychological harm that may be caused to doctors and/or nursing staff involved.

Jane says that she has been considering travelling to Switzerland where she has read on the Internet that they allow 'physician-assisted suicide'.

Q What is meant by the term 'physician-assisted suicide'? *1 mark*

1. EXAMPLE ANSWER

'An assisted suicide involves someone who has suicidal motives, intends to die, does something to cause his or her death, and is non-coerced [but] requires aid from a physician [who] can assist in a number of ways: by supplying information ... purchasing a weapon of self destruction, providing a lethal dose of pills or poison, giving encouragement ... or helping in the actual act of killing ...'

🛈 Physician-assisted suicide is not a form of euthanasia. With euthanasia the doctor rather than the patient is ultimately in control of ending the patient's life. However, with physician-assisted suicide the doctor does not directly bring about the death of the patient (or it would no longer be suicide), but does act in full awareness that they are enabling the patient to do so.

Weir, RF. 1992 The morality of physician-assisted suicide. *Law, Medicine and Health Care,* 20, 116–126

ⓘ Under current UK law a person cannot consent to his or her own death: this is generally considered to be murder. Assisting a person in their suicide is a statutory offence (under section 2 of the Suicide Act 1961), which carries a 14-year sentence or unlimited fine. Physician-assisted suicide is therefore currently illegal though there are moves to change the law: see Teaching notes below, on the Assisted Dying for the Terminally Ill Bill.

ⓘ Systems allowing physician-assisted suicide exist in Belgium and Switzerland as well as in the state of Oregon, USA.

Q List 3 arguments in favour of physician-assisted suicide over active euthanasia. ***3 marks***

1. **Physician-assisted suicide gives the patient final control over ending their life (as opposed to active euthanasia in which the final act is carried out by a doctor), increasing patient autonomy.**
2. **It would allow terminally ill patients who plan on committing suicide to delay it to a time when they are no longer physically capable of taking their own life unassisted, thus prolonging life.**
3. **Assisting suicide is morally better than actively taking life (see the Teaching notes on the acts/omissions doctrine below).**
4. **A system of physician-assisted suicide may be less open to misuse than one of active euthanasia.**

ⓘ The acts/omissions doctrine is used to justify passive over active euthanasia. It proposes that an act that brings about a bad outcome is morally worse than an omission that brings about this same outcome. So, applied to the euthanasia debate it infers that to act in a way that brings about the death of a patient (eg a lethal injection) is morally worse than to omit to do something that also brings about the death of a patient, eg antibiotic treatment.

🛈 The acts/omissions doctrine was referred to in the case of Tony Bland (see Scenario 5, Withholding and withdrawing treatment). In this case the judge determined that stopping artificial nutrition was failing to provide treatment that had previously been provided (an omission), rather than an act.

Q Briefly explain the doctrine of double effect and how this might relate to the administration of morphine during the dying phase.

2 marks

1. **It means that an action that brings about a foreseen bad effect may be justified if that bad outcome is an unintended side-effect of an action intended to bring about good.**

2. **It means that, if necessary, in giving an adequate dose of morphine to relieve the pain of a dying patient, it may be foreseen that this dose might cause the side-effect of shortening life.**

🛈 The doctrine of double effect argues that bad outcomes (eg death) may be morally justified if they are side-effects of actions performed with good motivation (eg the relief of pain).

🛈 The doctrine is recognised as legally valid. In the 1957 case of Dr Bodkin Adams, accused of murdering his patient by deliberately increasing doses of analgesia to life-threatening levels (*R* v *Adams* [1957] Crim. LR 365), the judge made the following statement during his summing up:

'If the first purpose of medicine – the restoration of health – could no longer be achieved, there was still much for the doctor to do, and he was entitled to do all that was proper and necessary to relieve pain and suffering even if the measures he took might incidentally shorten life by hours or even longer.'

🛈 Also, in oral evidence submitted to the Assisted Dying for the Terminally Ill Bill, the Attorney General stated in 2004 that it is not murder 'where a doctor acts to do all that is proper and necessary to relieve pain with the incidental effect that this

Euthanasia

will shorten a patient's life' (www.publications.parliament.uk).

❶ Many argue that the appropriate use of the range of drugs we now have available alleviates the need for reliance on the doctrine of double effect in symptom control at the end of life.

Total: *18 marks*

The following web sites make interesting and diametrically opposed reading:
Dignity in Dying: www.dignityindying.org.uk
ProLife Alliance: www.prolife.org.uk

Euthanasia

SCENARIO 3: EUTHANASIA AND ASSISTED DYING

TEACHING NOTES

Euthanasia and physician-assisted suicide are hot topics. Recent court cases and a change in the position of the British Medical Association to one of a neutral stance on assisted dying have maintained a high media profile for this topic. You should certainly understand the key arguments.

Arguments in favour of euthanasia

Various arguments for the legalisation of euthanasia are outlined in the answer section of this case above. Further detail is given below:

- *Relief of intolerable suffering (non-maleficence):*
  The argument is that the duty of doctors of non-maleficence (a duty to prevent harm) may justify euthanasia in order to prevent extreme distress.

- *Promotion of wellbeing and dignity (beneficence):*
  A system of legalised euthanasia would enable physicians to better aid their patients in maintaining dignity towards the end of life. This would fulfil a duty of beneficence (a duty to promote good), a moral obligation on all doctors.

- *Respect for autonomy (patient choice):*
  The arguments concerning autonomy are powerful ones. We live in a society in which choice and self-determination of our future are given high importance. Many believe that in failing to let patients with terminal disease choose their time of death we are failing to respect their autonomy.

- *Distributive justice:*
  Allows fair access to treatment for the majority, by restricting access to burdensome, life-prolonging or expensive treatments for a minority who are unlikely to derive benefit (eg a bed on the intensive care unit).

Arguments against euthanasia

- *Sanctity of life:*
  This might include religious and moral arguments. It holds that life is in itself inherently valuable and precious, that while someone is alive they have something that must be preserved by every means possible. While clearly this argument is one referred to in many world religions it should not be seen as just a religious argument. There are many people who believe that human life is special but who do not hold religious beliefs, and who believe that terminating human life is never justified.

- *The thin-end-of-the-wedge, or slippery-slope argument:*
  That if any limited form of euthanasia were legalised (eg voluntary euthanasia), this would lead to a descent into undesirable scenarios, either explicitly (eg a system of involuntary euthanasia) or covertly, with vulnerable patient groups (including those with incapacity) feeling pressured into accepting euthanasia.

- *Regulatory frameworks are difficult to police:*
  For example in the Netherlands, despite statutory safeguards and regulation, 1000 deaths annually (0.7% of the total) are ended by physicians without patient request.

- *Killing is a fundamental wrong for which there is no justification:*
  Again, it includes religious and moral arguments. That deliberately bringing about the end to someone's life is always immoral, even in the context of extreme suffering. In Christianity this may be seen as following the Ten Commandments: 'Thou shalt not kill.'

- *Loss of trust between patients, professionals and society in general.*

- *Society has a need to protect its most vulnerable members (the elderly, those with disability, those lacking mental capacity).*

- *Palliation provides a credible alternative:*
  It is argued that the provision of good palliative care for all would alleviate the need for euthanasia. There are also concerns that, were a formalised system of euthanasia to be introduced, palliative care services would suffer as they may take a lower political priority. In the Netherlands, where legalised euthanasia exists, it has been suggested that palliative care facilities have failed to develop at the same rate as in other European countries with similar economic power.

The Assisted Dying for the Terminally Ill Bill

Assisted Dying for the Terminally Ill Bill [HL], HL Bill 36, 2005; www.publications.parliament.uk (Last accessed March 2006).

Also known as the Joffe Bill (after Lord Joffe, who initially put the bill before the House of Lords), this proposes a legalised system of physician-assisted suicide. Were it to become law, it would 'enable an adult who has capacity and who is suffering unbearably as a result of a terminal illness to receive medical assistance to die at his own considered and persistent request; and for connected purposes.'

This bill recommends a change to section 2 of the Suicide Act 1961 (c. 60), in order to make it legal for a third party to assist a person to commit suicide under the terms as stated in the Assisted Dying for the Terminally Ill Bill.

As such it would be legal for a doctor to prescribe medication to a patient in order for them to end their own life, subject to the conditions summarised below. Where a patient is unable to take an oral medicine, the doctor will be allowed to 'prescribe and provide' the means to allow them to self-administer that fatal drug.

Euthanasia

- There must be a written and signed request from the patient.

- The doctor must be sure that the patient has capacity.

- The doctor must be satisfied that the patient is terminally ill, with a prognosis of less than 6 months, and that they are enduring extreme suffering as a result of that illness.

- The patient must have been fully informed as to their disease and its prognosis, the options provided by palliative care, and what will occur should they choose assisted dying.

- The patient must be encouraged to tell their relatives of their wish to be assisted to die.

- A second physician must also ensure all of the above.

- The patient must also be aware of their right to change their mind at any time.

Important cases

Diane Pretty v the United Kingdom
Pretty v the United Kingdom – 2346/02 [2002] ECHR 427

Summary

- Diane Pretty was a 43-year-old woman who suffered from motor neurone disease.

- Greatly incapacitated by her disease (paralysed from the neck down and artificially fed), Diane took the decision that when she judged her condition unbearable she wished to have the option of taking her own life. This would require assistance from a third party.

- In July 2001 Diane wrote to the Director of Public Prosecutions (DPP) asking him to give an undertaking not to prosecute her husband should he assist her to commit suicide in accordance with her wishes. This request was refused, on the grounds that the DPP could not authorise an illegal act, whatever the circumstances.

- Diane sought judicial review of this decision first at the Divisional Court and then the House of Lords. She lost both cases.

- In March 2002, Diane's case was heard at the European Court of Human Rights where she 'alleged that the refusal of the DPP to grant an immunity from prosecution to her husband if he assisted her in committing suicide and the prohibition in domestic law on assisting suicide infringed her rights under articles 2, 3, 8, 9 and 14 of the Human Rights Act.

Judgment

- The European Court of Human Rights found that there had been no violation of Diane Pretty's Human Rights under the articles cited.

- They ruled that Diane Pretty could not interpret article 2 (a right to life) as a right to death.

Diane Pretty died on 11 May 2002, after 10 days of breathing difficulties caused by motor neurone disease.

Euthanasia

Glass v the United Kingdom

Glass v the United Kingdom – 61827/00 [2004] ECHR 103

Summary

- David Glass was a child with severe mental and physical handicap.

- In 1998 he became very unwell and required surgery to relieve respiratory difficulties. Following this he encountered post-operative problems and required admission to ITU and time on a ventilator. He was eventually discharged home, but had several re-admissions with respiratory tract infections.

- On another admission David was believed to be dying by the medical team, who wished to give him morphine to relieve his distress. David's mother did not agree he was dying, and did not want morphine to be given, believing it would compromise his chances of recovery.

- It was stressed by the medical team that the administration of morphine was not intended to kill the first applicant but to relieve his distress; 'use of Morphine is **not** euthanasia – it is to relieve [David's] distress...'

- Morphine was given against the mother's wishes; he was also placed under a DNR order without consultation with his mother. Relations with medical staff deteriorated to the point where a fight broke out, and staff were injured.

- David's mother applied for judicial review of the decisions of the health care trust with regard to her son. She failed, and her application to the Court of Appeal was refused.

- David's mother took the case to the European Court of Human Rights, arguing that that the government had failed to respect David's right to a private and family life under article 8 of the Human Rights Act.

Judgment

- The Court judged David's mother to be acting as his legal proxy, with 'authority to action his behalf and to defend his interests, including in the area of medical treatment'.

- It found that 'the decision to impose treatment on the first applicant in defiance of the second applicant's objections gave rise to an interference with the first applicant's right to respect for his private life, and in particular his right to physical integrity'.

- The Court decided there had been a breach of the Human Rights Act under article 8 and awarded damages totalling ☐25,000 to David's mother.

 These judgments can be read at the World Legal Information Institute (www.worldlii.org).

Euthanasia

SCENARIO 4: ANTENATAL SCREENING AND ABORTION

ANSWERS

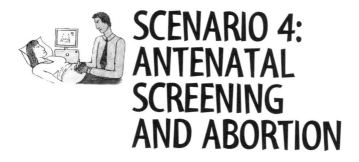

SCENARIO 4: ANTENATAL SCREENING AND ABORTION

Hannah, a 38-year-solicitor, attends her local obstetric outpatients for her antenatal care. Because of her age she is offered a screening test for Down's syndrome.

Q What information should you give Hannah about the screening test? **4 marks**

1. **What the screening test involves.**

2. **The possibility of false-positive and false-negative results.**

3. **That a positive screening test is not the same as a positive diagnosis.**

4. **The further investigations that may be necessary to confirm the diagnosis if the test is positive.**

5. **What the options are for treatment: with Down's syndrome the only two real options are to terminate the pregnancy or continue to term but some conditions detected in utero may be treatable.**

 Any counselling regarding a screening test must be non-directive, ie the doctor must not impose their own views, so that the woman or couple can make their own informed decision, which includes the right not to have the screening test.

QUESTIONS
PAGES 19–24

🔴 Screening for Down's syndrome can take place in the first or second trimesters using a combination of serum screening tests with or without nuchal translucency (NT) measured by ultrasound. The results from these tests are combined with the woman's age and gestation of the fetus to calculate the risk of having a child with Down's syndrome; those at high risk are offered either chorionic villus sampling or amniocentesis, from which a diagnosis of trisomy 21 can be made.

Q Give 3 advantages and 3 disadvantages of antenatal screening. **6 marks**

Advantages:

1. Screening increases the reproductive choices of families at risk of affected pregnancies.
2. Some conditions identified through antenatal screening can be treated in utero.
3. A pregnant woman has the right to know if her pregnancy is at risk.
4. Terminating affected pregnancies reduces future suffering.

Disadvantages:

1. Screening for particular abnormalities may encourage prejudice towards individuals already born with that condition.
2. No screening test is 100% sensitive and specific. False-positives can lead to unnecessary worry and further investigation; false-negatives can lead to false reassurance and missed opportunity for diagnosis.
3. Screening may reduce parental choice because of the expectation that mothers with a positive test will terminate their pregnancy.
4. Screening may be used to identify pregnancies with 'conditions' for which termination is unjustified, eg gender.

The screening test is positive and amniocentesis confirms that her baby has Down's syndrome. She is distraught and requests an abortion.

Q Outline the legal frameworks that govern abortion in the UK.   *2 marks*

1. **The Abortion Act 1967.**

2. **Human Fertilisation and Embryology Act 1990 (which amended the above Act).**

🛈 These two Acts regulate abortion in England, Scotland and Wales. They do not extend to Northern Ireland, where abortion is governed by the Offences Against the Person Act 1861, which makes it an offence to 'procure a miscarriage unlawfully'. There is still no guidance to date on what would constitute a lawful abortion in Northern Ireland.

🛈 Of the 200,000 abortions carried out in England, Scotland and Wales every year, approximately 5% are undertaken for non-residents (mainly from Northern Ireland and the Irish Republic).

Q Up to what gestational age could Hannah's pregnancy be legally terminated due to Down's syndrome?   *1 mark*

1. **Up to birth.**

🛈 The term 'abortion' refers to an induced termination of an established pregnancy (ie after implantation) up to birth.

🛈 The Act allows pregnancies to be legally terminated up to birth if there is a substantial risk that the child would be 'seriously handicapped'. Only 1% of abortions are carried out for fetal abnormality (see Teaching notes). The Act does not give any guidance about how 'serious handicap' should be defined, however (though Down's syndrome would be considered a serious handicap – see Teaching notes).

95

🛈 Reverend Joanna Jepson sought a legal review of the decision by the West Mercia Police Force not to prosecute two doctors who had terminated a pregnancy after 24 weeks where the fetus had been diagnosed with bilateral cleft lip and palate. She contended that this did not constitute a 'serious handicap' and therefore the abortion had been unlawful (she herself had been born with a jaw defect). The police reinvestigated the case and sent the file to the Crown Prosecution Service (CPS). Subsequently the CPS decided not to prosecute the doctors, saying that they had decided in good faith that there was a substantial risk that the child would be seriously handicapped if born (*Jepson* v *The Chief Constable of West Mercia Police Constabulary* [2003] EWHC 3318)

🛈 Approximately 95% of women with a positive diagnosis of Down's syndrome opt to terminate their pregnancy.

Q List 3 legal criteria for abortion other than fetal abnormality.

3 marks

1. *The continuance of the pregnancy would involve risk, greater than if the pregnancy were terminated, of injury to the physical or mental health of the pregnant woman or any existing children:* the emphasis here is on preventing harm to the woman and her family.

2. *The termination is necessary to prevent grave permanent injury to the physical or mental health of the pregnant woman:* the emphasis here is on preventing serious harm to the woman.

3. *The continuance of the pregnancy would involve risk to the life of the pregnant woman, greater than if the pregnancy were terminated:* the emphasis here is clearly on saving the woman's life.

🟦 When it is because of fetal abnormality, to prevent grave permanent injury or to save the woman's life, the pregnancy may be legally terminated up to birth. When terminating the pregnancy because of criterion 1 (the main ground cited for terminating pregnancies) the pregnancy may only be legally terminated up to 24 weeks of gestation. This upper limit was set on the basis of fetal viability, ie the time after which the fetus can survive outside the womb. One of the arguments for reviewing the abortion time limits is that because of medical advances it is claimed that fetuses are now viable before 24 weeks (see Teaching notes).

Q What legal right does Hannah's partner have in her decision to terminate the pregnancy?   *1 mark*

1. None.

🟦 The Abortion Act gives no rights to fathers; they cannot force a woman to have an abortion or stop her from having an abortion. In fact there is no legal obligation for the woman (or medical practitioners) to involve the father in the decision.

🟦 More controversial is whether competent minors (<16 years old) can consent to an abortion without their parents' knowledge. Legally, minors who are 'Gillick competent' can consent to treatment but cannot refuse it. This principle was established in a case brought, and ultimately lost, by Mrs Gillick against her local health authority in which she wanted to prevent her daughters receiving contraceptive and abortion advice and treatment without her knowledge and consent (this is discussed in greater depth in Scenario 2, Consent in minors).

Antenatal Screening

Q What are the wider implications for society of abortion on request? *3 marks*

1. **May promote irresponsible attitudes to unprotected sex, eg leading to a rise in sexually transmitted infections.**

2. **May encourage prejudice towards people with a handicap.**

3. **May reduce society's respect for the unborn child, eg it may become less socially unacceptable to drink/smoke during pregnancy.**

ⓘ In some countries (eg Canada and Germany) abortion is 'available on request' up to certain gestational limits. It is not 'available on request' in the UK though some argue that the legal criteria (principally criterion 1) are so loosely interpreted that to all intents and purposes it is.

ⓘ What are your views on abortion? Do you believe abortion should be 'available on request'? Do you think the 24-week upper limit should be raised, scrapped or lowered?

Total: *20 marks*

SCENARIO 4: ANTENATAL SCREENING AND ABORTION

 TEACHING NOTES

In England, Scotland and Wales, abortion is governed by the Abortion Act 1967 (as amended by the Human Fertilisation and Embryology Act 1990). This law does not extend to Northern Ireland where abortion is governed by the Offences Against the Person Act 1861, which makes it an offence to 'procure a miscarriage unlawfully'. There is still no guidance to date on what would constitute a lawful abortion in Northern Ireland.

The Abortion Act permits the termination of pregnancy, by a registered medical practitioner, in an NHS hospital or approved premises, if two registered medical practitioners (only one in a medical emergency) certify that one of the following legal criteria apply[1]:

1. **The pregnancy has not exceeded its 24th week and the continuance of the pregnancy would involve risk, greater than if the pregnancy were terminated, of injury to the physical or mental health of the pregnant woman or any existing children.**

2. **The termination is necessary to prevent grave permanent injury to the physical or mental health of the pregnant woman.**

3. **The continuance of the pregnancy would involve risk to the life of the pregnant woman, greater than if the pregnancy were terminated.**

[1]British Medical Association (BMA) *The Law and ethics of abortion*. BMA views 1999 (available at www.bma.org.uk Last accessed February 2006)

4. **There is substantial risk that if the child were born he or she would suffer from such physical or mental abnormalities as to be seriously handicapped.**

The Act includes a conscientious objection clause, which allows doctors to refuse to participate in abortions (except in an emergency). However, they are required to refer patients to other practitioners without delay.

The Chief Medical Officer (CMO) must be notified of any termination of pregnancy within 7 days. Information provided includes the gestational age, the grounds for terminating the pregnancy, the method of termination and any resulting complications. Abortion statistics are published annually using data derived from these notifications and are summarised below[2]:

- Approximately 200,000 abortions were performed, of which 9000 were undertaken for non-residents (mainly from Northern Ireland and the Irish Republic).

- 95% of abortions were carried out within 24 weeks on the grounds that continuance of pregnancy involved risk of injury to the physical or mental health of the woman.

- Approximately 90% of abortions were carried out at less than 13 weeks of gestation and 60% under 10 weeks.

- 1% of abortions were carried out due to fetal abnormality: 95% of these were carried out before 24 weeks (majority between 13 and 19 weeks); only 5% were performed after 24 weeks (the main reason for late abortion is time of diagnosis).

- The majority of abortions (> 95%) beyond 24 weeks are due to fetal abnormality.

[2]British Medical Association (BMA). *Abortion time limits*. BMA briefing paper 2005 (available at www.bma.org.uk Last accessed February 2006)

Criteria 2–4 permit termination of the pregnancy up to term; criterion 1, as stated, permits termination up to 24 weeks of gestation. The upper limit of 24 weeks was made on the basis of fetal viability, ie the time after which the fetus can survive outside the womb. It is claimed that because of medical advances fetuses are now viable before 24 weeks though this view is not supported by the EPICure study[3] (and this is not taking into account any associated disability in the children who survived).

Gestation (weeks)	% Survival to discharge
21	0
22	1
23	11
24	26
25	44

Fetal abnormalities may be diagnosed at any stage of gestation, for example during routine ultrasound scans at 10–13 weeks and at 18–20 weeks, following amniocentesis or chorionic villous sampling (CVS), or following non-routine scans due to concerns regarding the pregnancy. However, the Act does not give any guidance about how serious handicap should be defined. The Royal College of Obstetricians and Gynaecologists (RCOG) have set out guidance on what should be considered when assessing whether fetal abnormalities constitute a serious handicap[4]:

[3]Costeloe K., Gibson, AT., Marlow, N., Wilkinson, AR. (2000). The EPICure Study: outcome to discharge from hospital for babies born at the threshold of viability. *Paediatrics,* 106, 659–671

[4]Royal College of Obstetricians and Gynaecologists (RCOG). *Termination of pregnancy for foetal abnormality in England, Wales and Scotland.* London: RCOG Press, 1996

1. The probability of effective treatment, either in utero or after birth.

2. The probable degree of self-awareness and of ability to communicate with others.

3. The suffering that would be experienced.

4. The extent to which actions essential for health that normal individuals perform unaided would have to be provided by others.

5. The probability of being able to live alone and to be self-supporting as an adult.

The abortion statistics show that only 1% of all abortions are due to *fetal abnormalities. The vast majority of these are carried out before 24 weeks.* A small minority are carried out after this time, principally due to the timing of the diagnosis, eg cardiac defects are best diagnosed at 24 weeks.

Abortion is a complex issue (both legally and ethically) and as such there are a wide range of views, which can be broadly classified into:

- **Pro-life:** belief that the fetus should have the same rights as a person and therefore abortion is morally equivalent to killing a human being. This was subject to a recent challenge in the European Court of Human Rights in that Article 2 (right to life) of the Human Rights Act should extend to the unborn though the Court rejected this. (*Vo* v *France* (2005) 40 EHRR 12.)

- **Pro-choice:** belief that until birth the fetus is not a separate being but rather a part of the mother's body; therefore it is the woman's rights that are relevant and not the interests of the fetus.

- **Gradualist approach:** belief that as the fetus develops it gains more rights and therefore the justification required for terminating the pregnancy needs to be greater.

The four main areas of contention relate to: (1) abortion on request, (2) the moral status of the fetus, (3) abortion time limits and (4) the ability of competent minors to consent to abortion (which continues to be the subject of legal challenges and is discussed in greater detail in Scenario 2, Consent in minors):

- Pro-life groups argue that criterion 1 is so loosely interpreted by medical practitioners that it already amounts to 'abortion on request'.

- The moral status of the fetus refers to those stages of development which are considered morally significant (and hence confer certain if not full human rights). At one end of the spectrum is the view that fertilisation (or implantation) marks the stage at which human life acquires full moral status. A variation on this is that the embryo should be viewed as a 'potential person' and hence afforded the same moral status as other human beings. In keeping with these views, fetal abnormality, however severe, would not justify abortion since this would be morally equivalent to killing a disabled child or adult. For some, the fetus achieves moral status when it is capable of independent existence (fetal viability is discussed above). For others, birth is seen as the morally significant stage.

- There have been calls to lower the upper gestational age limit for abortion from 24 weeks on the basis of both fetal viability and restricting 'abortion on request'. Pro-choice groups argue that the majority of abortions carried out on the grounds of criterion 1 occur before 13 weeks and therefore lowering of the age limit would have little effect on these abortions but would impact significantly if applied to abortions for fetal abnormalities where late diagnosis is often unavoidable; other reasons for late abortions include delay in seeking abortion due to personal circumstances, failure to recognise the pregnancy earlier and difficulty in accessing abortion services.

Antenatal Screening

SCENARIO 5:
WITHHOLDING AND WITHDRAWING TREATMENT

ANSWERS

SCENARIO 5: WITHHOLDING AND WITHDRAWING TREATMENT

Maeve is an 80-year-old woman admitted to A&E from a nursing home and is barely conscious on arrival. She has a past medical history of Alzheimer's disease, diabetes, hypertension, rheumatoid arthritis, chronic renal failure and a previous stroke. On this occasion she is found to be suffering from pneumonia and dehydration, and tests show evidence of a recent myocardial infarction (MI). Her carer tells you that Maeve has little quality of life; she is in constant pain, is unable to interact meaningfully with others, is frequently very distressed and eats and drinks little.

Q What is meant by the term 'active treatment'?   ***1 mark***

1. **Treatments that prolong life/postpone death.**

ⓘ 'Active treatment' refers to treatments that postpone death, eg renal dialysis, CPR, antibiotics, chemotherapy, and artificial nutrition/hydration.

ⓘ The term 'basic care' is used to describe those treatments that do not prolong life, eg nursing care, symptom control (including relief of pain and distress) and the provision of oral hydration and nutrition.

QUESTIONS
PAGES 25–30

107

Q List 4 arguments for and 4 arguments against withdrawal of active treatment in this situation. *8 marks*

For:

1. **The treatment may only prolong the dying process.**

2. **The treatment may cause suffering that is disproportionate to the benefit likely to result.**

3. **That her quality of life is such that it should not be prolonged.**

4. **A decision not to treat may afford the patient greater dignity at the end of life.**

5. **The resources may be better used for other patients (this becomes especially relevant if intensive care is to be considered).**

Against:

1. **Sanctity of life (ie all life has intrinsic value).**

2. **That assessment of quality of life may be unreliable (especially where the patient cannot express a view).**

3. **Prognostic difficulties.**

4. **Religious objections.**

5. **That it may cause distress to relatives.**

Maeve's daughter arrives. She feels that her mother would not have wanted to be treated for this illness.

Q Describe 2 other ways in which you might ascertain a patient's wishes with regard to withholding/withdrawing treatment. *2 marks*

1. **Where the patient is competent their views must always be sought.**

108

2. **A statement made in advance (a so-called 'advance directive', verbal or written) by the patient, when competent, about how they would wish to be treated in the present circumstances.**

3. **Talking to other people close to the patient, eg friends, their GP. They may recall verbal advance statements by the patient about how they would wish to be treated.**

4. **The patient's notes; previous wishes of the patient may have been recorded.**

● You have a responsibility to try to obtain information as to the views of the patient, including making a reasonable effort to check if an advance directive exists (you do not have to delay treatment to look for an advance directive where there is no evidence that one exists).

● Advance refusals of treatment carry the same legal weight as contemporaneous refusals, providing the refusal relates to the circumstances presenting now and was fully informed.

Q List 2 steps that may be taken in the event that relatives and doctors strongly disagree about the decision to withhold/withdraw active treatment from a patient who lacks capacity. *2 marks*

1. **Obtaining a second and independent clinical opinion.**

2. **Legal advice regarding whether a court order is required.**

● Ideally, a consensus should be reached between all health care professionals involved with a patient and their relatives to withdraw/withhold treatment. If this cannot be achieved, the GMC recommends that a second opinion or independent review should be sought. If strong disagreement still remains, legal advice should be obtained as to whether a court order is necessary.

❶ In a situation where a member of staff disagrees with a consensus decision to withdraw/withhold treatment, alternative arrangements for care should be made, enabling that member of staff not to have to participate.

Q Can a competent patient insist that life-prolonging treatment be provided? *1 mark*

1. No.

❶ Currently there is no legal obligation for doctors to provide life-prolonging treatment where they do not believe it to be either necessary or in the best interests of the patient (though this may be open to challenge under the Human Rights Act 1998, www.opsi.gov.uk).

Maeve is admitted to the medical assessment unit where she is reviewed by the on-call consultant who agrees with the family's wish that Maeve should not be given antibiotics.

Q List 4 responsibilities you have following the decision to withhold treatment. *4 marks*

1. You must inform all those with a legitimate interest in the care and welfare of the patient.

2. The decision must be recorded clearly in the patient's clinical record.

3. You should plan when to review this decision if appropriate.

4. A care plan should be made for the patient, including the ongoing provision of basic and palliative care.

5. The provision of support and counselling to the patient's family.

Maeve's condition declines rapidly over the next few hours and she is now clearly dying. It becomes difficult to insert an intravenous drip to maintain hydration.

Q Can the medical team legally withdraw artificial hydration?

1 mark

1. Yes.

🛈 Artificial nutrition and hydration means nutrition and hydration provided by a means that is not the oral route. Examples include feeding via a nasogastric (NG) or percutaneous endoscopic gastrostomy (PEG) tube, and fluid via an intravenous cannula.

🛈 There is no legal preclusion to withdrawing artificial nutrition and hydration where death is imminent and where continuing it is felt not to be either necessary or in the best interests of the patient. Artificial nutrition and hydration may also be withdrawn under other circumstances – more detail is given in the Teaching notes for this scenario.

🛈 There is no legal difference between withholding and withdrawing a treatment. Where uncertainty exists, treatments should not be withheld just because the medical team are worried about having to withdraw it later.

Total: *19 marks*

Withholding Treatment

SCENARIO 5: WITHHOLDING AND WITHDRAWING TREATMENT

TEACHING NOTES

The GMC guidance on withdrawing and withholding treatment can be read at: www.gmc-uk.org.

BMA Guidance on end-of-life decision making, including treatment withdrawal, is detailed on their website (www.bma.org.uk).

Following several prominent English court cases, the issue of withdrawal of treatment is a topical one. It is essential that all clinicians have a clear understanding of both the ethical and legal issues that underlie treatment withholding and withdrawal.

As with consent, the easiest way to break this topic down is to think of it in terms of those patients who are competent, and those who are incompetent (see Scenario 6, Consent in adults, for more detail as to how this is assessed).

Competent adults

Where the patient decides to refuse treatment

- As explained in Scenario 6, Consent in adults, any competent adult has an absolute right to refuse treatment.

- The right to refuse treatment has been upheld on numerous occasions in UK courts, and is also protected under the Human Rights Act 1998.

- Contemporaneous refusals (statements from the patient at the time) and advance refusals (eg a valid advance directive) carry the same legal weight, and must be treated as such. More information on this can be found in Scenario 1, Advance directives.

- This absolute right includes refusal of life-prolonging treatment; a patient can decline treatment even where death will certainly result. This includes artificial nutrition and hydration.

- The treating clinician has a duty to offer enough information to ensure that a patient's decision to withdraw treatment is informed; this will include pros and cons of treatment, any alternatives, and the potential outcomes if treatment is provided or withheld.

- Even if a patient refuses the offer of information, their decision to withdraw treatment must be respected.

- Where members of the medical team disagree with the decision to withdraw treatment, they can explain their concerns, but must not put the patient under pressure to relent and continue treatment.

Where the medical team decides to withdraw treatment

- Where a medical team feels that withdrawal of life-prolonging treatment is in the best interests of a competent patient, eg to stop chemotherapy, the decision not to continue treatment should be first discussed with that patient.

- Where the patient disagrees with that decision, careful discussion of the views of all those involved should take place but ultimately the medical team are not under any legal obligation to continue life-prolonging treatment when they do not feel it is appropriate (there are extra safeguards concerning artificial nutrition and hydration – see below).

Withholding Treatment

- Where patient and doctor disagree, a second clinical opinion should be sought.

- Where treatment such as artificial nutrition and hydration is keeping a patient alive and the patient wishes it to continue, doctors may not withdraw. This was confirmed in the Burke judgement, which went (for full legal reference see teaching notes) as far as to say any doctor that does so is guilty of murder. This applies to advance as well as contemporaneous requests for artificial nutrition and hydration to continue.

- Where death is imminent, and thus artificial nutrition and hydration will not prolong life, a doctor may withdraw this treatment if he or she believes it to be causing more harm than good, even given an advance/contemporaneous request for it to continue.

Incompetent adults

- As with all decisions to withhold or withdraw treatment, the best possible medical evidence as to the diagnosis and its prognosis should be used.

- Detailed consideration of the benefits and burdens of treatment should be undertaken by all those health care professionals involved in the patient's care.

- It is legally possible to withdraw/withhold treatment that is considered to be unnecessary and to provide no benefit to the patient.

- The sort of factors that might be taken into consideration in assessing quality of life include an ability to interact with others, an awareness of oneself, and an ability to gain enjoyment from activities.

ⓘ See the BMA publication, *Withholding and withdrawing life-prolonging medical treatment: guidance for decision making*, 2nd ed. (2001) for more detail on this subject

- Reasonable effort should be made to establish whether a patient has given any advance indication as to their wishes in such a situation, eg an advance directive and records of conversations with other health care professionals.

- The views of the person's relatives should be sought, as should their knowledge of the patient's wishes when competent.

- Where relatives and doctors disagree significantly as to what is in the patient's best interests, a second opinion should be sought. Failing this, legal advice should be requested as to whether a court order is required.

- In the case of a patient in a persistent vegetative state, it is advisable to seek a court declaration of lawfulness prior to withdrawal of life-sustaining treatment (see *Airedale NHS Trust v Bland* overleaf).

- The senior clinician looking after the patient, ie the patient's consultant, should make the final decision to withdraw/withhold treatment.

- Basic care should always be provided.

Withholding Treatment

Important cases

Airedale NHS Trust v *Bland*

Airedale NHS Trust v *Bland* [1993] AC 789; [1993] 1 All ER 821; [1993] 1 FLR 1026; (1993) 12 BMLR 64

Summary

- Concerns the case of Tony Bland a 17-year-old victim of the Hillsborough disaster.

- He was left in a persistent vegetative state, after crush injuries prevented him from breathing and caused brain injury.

- After 3 years the hospital went to court requesting that they might terminate life-prolonging treatment, including artificial hydration and nutrition. They also sought assurance that when death occurred, they would not be held legally responsible.

Judgment

- The House of Lords agreed with the request, ruling that artificial nutrition and hydration were medical treatments, and that discontinuing them was legal.

- The judges decided that the withdrawal of artificial hydration and nutrition should be considered an omission (to fail to do something you have previously done) rather than an act; therefore, murder would not have been committed.

- They stressed the importance of taking into consideration the previous wishes of the patient and the views of their family.

- They advised that in other situations where doctors wish to withdraw artificial nutrition and hydration from patients diagnosed with persistent vegetative state, court rulings should also be sought.

Withholding Treatment

Burke v *General Medical Council*

R (on the application of Burke) v *General Medical Council & ors*
[2005] EWCA Civ 1003

Summary

- Leslie Burke, aged 45 years at the time of the case, suffered from spinocerebellar ataxia – an inherited degenerative neurological condition that causes increasing physical disability until the point of death.

- Patients with spinocerebellar ataxia retain full mental awareness.

- Mr Burke was aware that at some point he would need artificial nutrition and hydration, and wished this to continue until he died from natural causes.

- He was worried that doctors might decide his life was not worth living, and withdraw artificial hydration and nutrition before the point of natural death. He claimed that GMC guidance to doctors on withdrawing and withholding treatment was unlawful as he argued it allowed this.

- Leslie Burke initially won his case, but the judgment was later overturned at appeal (case reference above).

Judgment

- The Court of Appeal found that the GMC guidance was lawful.

- They judged that the GMC guidance allowed withdrawal of artificial nutrition and hydration only where it was considered clinically inappropriate. The Court felt that as administering treatment necessary to keep a patient alive could not be clinically inappropriate, Mr Burke's fears were unwarranted.

 These cases can be read at the British and Irish Legal Information Institute (www.bailii.org).

Withholding Treatment

SCENARIO 6:
CONSENT IN ADULTS

ANSWERS

SCENARIO 6: CONSENT IN ADULTS

Catherine is an 83-year-old woman who was admitted from home following a collapse. She has been very fit and well her whole life, except that over the last few months she has been suffering increasingly with chest pain and breathlessness. After several tests it is discovered that she has severe aortic stenosis (a serious problem with one of the valves in her heart). Despite optimal medical treatment she continues to remain symptomatic and a decision must be made about surgical management. She has no other significant medical history but does report being 'a little forgetful at times'.

Q Outline 3 ethical arguments for obtaining valid consent for treatment in adults. **3 marks**

1. **Respect for autonomous choice.**

2. **Avoidance of intentional harm, including protection from unwanted interference by others.**

3. **Promotion of wellbeing and benefit based on a full understanding of the available options for treatment (beneficence).**

❶ In English law, any treatment carried out on an adult without their valid consent could give rise to civil or criminal proceedings in battery (non-consensual touching).

❶ There are rare examples of clinicians being sued for battery, eg *Devi* v *West Midlands RHA* [1980] CLY 687. In this case a 29-year-old Sikh woman successfully sued her surgeon for battery when an operation to repair a ruptured uterus resulted in her sterilisation (a hysterectomy was performed). She argued that she would not have consented to this as she wanted two more children.

❶ More commonly, doctors failing to provide adequate information about a treatment have been subject to a civil action in negligence.

Q Which 3 conditions must be met in order for consent to be legally valid? ***3 marks***

1. Consent must be informed.

2. The person must have capacity.

3. The consent must be given freely (not under duress).

❶ In order for consent to be informed, the patient must be provided with adequate information in a form they can understand in order to allow them to make a reasoned decision. This should include information about the illness and treatment, side-effects and alternatives.

 Detailed guidelines about the sort of information that should be provided are given on the GMC website (www.gmc-uk.org).

Catherine tells you that she is keen to pursue surgery but she would like to know a few more facts, in particular if it is possible that she might die during the operation.

Q Do you have to inform Catherine about all the possible risks of her surgery? **_1 mark_**

1. No.

🛈 To avoid battery it is necessary only to give the 'nature and purpose' of the proposed treatment.[1] To avoid negligence, the doctor has a duty to disclose sufficient information to allow the patient to make an informed choice about their treatment (This is covered in the case of _Sidaway_ v _Board of Governors of Bethlem Royal Hospital_ [1985] AC 871; [1985] 1 All ER 643 (HL)). For more detail on the implementation of this in practice see the Teaching notes for this scenario.

🛈 There are 3 generally accepted technical measures of how much information is enough:

- **The professional practice standard** – this is also known as the 'Bolam test' (_Bolam_ v _Friern Hospital Management Committee_ [1957] 1WLR 582). 'The test is the standard of the ordinary skilled man exercising and professing to have that special skill.' Basically, the amount of information given should be the same as given by other doctors who perform that procedure.

- **The reasonable person standard** – for information to be judged sufficient, it must be enough to allow a 'reasonable person' to make an informed decision about the proposed treatment/procedure, ie the amount a 'reasonable person' would wish to know.

[1]Considered in the legal case _Chatterton_ v _Gerson_ [1981] QB 432; [1981] 1 All ER 257 (QBD) as per Bristow J: '...once the patient is informed in broad terms of the nature of the procedure which is intended, and gives her consent, that consent is real.'

123

- **The patient rights standard** – the amount of information that is acceptable should be based on telling the patient everything they wish to know.

Q List 3 legally acceptable forms of consent to medical treatment.

3 marks

1. **Written consent.**

2. **Verbal consent.**

3. **Implied consent.**

❶ Implied consent concerns action taken by a patient that indicates consent to a treatment or procedure, eg opening their mouth to allow their temperature to be taken.

❶ There is no legal requirement for consent to treatment to be written. However, it is expected (including in professional guidelines) that written consent should be obtained for complex treatments and procedures, those with any serious risks and those for which there is a research rather than a therapeutic interest. It also makes it a whole lot easier to prove what was said should it end up in court!

❶ All forms of consent carry the same legal status; the difference relates to the subsequent justification that consent was given and valid. Equally, a signed consent form does not of itself prove consent to be legally valid.

Catherine's family confront you, furious that you have allowed Catherine to agree to surgery 'at her age'.

Q Give 3 conditions that must be met for an adult to be deemed to have capacity to consent to medical treatment. **3 marks**

1. **The person must be able to understand and retain the information provided about the illness/treatment.**[4]

2. **They must believe the information provided.**

3. **The person must be able to process or weigh-up the information provided.**

4. **The person must be able to communicate the decision.**

🛈 The first element above was recognised in the case of *Re C (adult: refusal of medical treatment)* [1994] 1 All ER 819 (Fam Div)

🛈 The belief element was given less emphasis in the subsequent Appeal Court case *Re MB (adult: medical treatment)* (1997) 38 BMLR 175 (CA).

🛈 It is worth bearing in mind that decisions about treatment do not have to be wise. A seemingly foolhardy decision does not automatically translate into lack of capacity. You can not decide a patient lacks capacity simply because you do not think the decision is in their best interests.

 The Mental Capacity Act 2005 makes the conditions above statutorily defined (read at www.opsi.gov.uk) This is likely to come into force in 2007.

Q List 2 situations in which consent to treatment is not legally required in adults. **2 marks**

1. **Where an adult lacks capacity, including in an emergency when consent cannot be obtained – but the treatment must be limited to that necessary to preserve life.**

Consent in Adults

2. **Mental illness – under certain circumstances a person with mental illness may be treated without their consent for that illness only under the terms of the Mental Health Act 1983.**

In English law no adult can consent for another (until the Mental Capacity Act 2005 takes full effect) and so some other justification should be found. These are the common law principles of necessity and best interests. There is a presumption of capacity in adults but it is one that may be rebutted. Once found to be incapable of making a legally valid decision there is a principle of continuance: ie incapacity persists until reassessment establishes that the patient has regained capacity.

Q List 4 factors which, legally or ethically, you should take into consideration when deciding to treat a patient who lacks capacity for decision making. *4 marks*

1. **Is the determination of incapacity correct?**

2. **Is it safe to delay treatment until capacity is regained?**

3. **Is there a valid advance refusal (directive) of treatment?**

4. **Is the treatment necessary (considering the urgency of treatment and the range of possible interventions, together with their likely outcomes, risks and benefits)?**

5. **Is the treatment in the patient's best interests (involves weighing the interests a patient might have in receiving and not receiving a given treatment; weighing up the burdens and benefits of treatment)?**

6. **The views of all those with a legitimate interest in that patient's welfare, including relatives. (This is explicit from the Glass judgement: *Glass* v *UK*; see Scenario 3, Euthanasia and assisted dying for more information on this case.)**

● GMC guidelines list the following factors that must be taken into consideration when treating in the best interests of an adult who lacks capacity[2]:

- Treatment/investigation options that are clinically indicated.

- Any evidence of the patient's previously expressed preferences, including an advance statement.

- Your own and the health care team's knowledge of the patient's background, such as cultural, religious, or employment considerations.

- Views about the patient's preferences given by a third party who may have other knowledge of the patient, for example the patient's partner, family, carer, tutor-dative (Scotland), or a person with parental responsibility.

- Which option least restricts the patient's future choices, where more than one option (including non-treatment) seems reasonable in the patient's best interest.

● If a patient refuses treatment when they have capacity to do so, it is not reasonable to proceed with treatment if that patient ceases to have capacity (eg becomes unconscious).

Q Can Catherine's family overrule her legally valid agreement to treatment? *1 mark*

1. **No.**

● Relatives cannot refuse treatment on behalf of an adult relative, although where no consensus on best interests can be reached it may be necessary to seek a court opinion.

Total: **20 marks**

Consent in Adults

---

[2]GMC *Seeking patients' consent: the ethical considerations.* 1998. (available at www.gmc-uk.org Last accessed April 2006)

SCENARIO 6: CONSENT IN ADULTS

TEACHING NOTES

Every human being of adult years and sound mind has a right to determine what shall be done with his own body; and a surgeon who performs an operation without his patient's consent commits an assault.

Schloendorff v *Society of New York Hospital* 105 NE 92 (NY, 1914)

You must have a firm understanding of the issues surrounding consent in adults; you will be dealing with this day in, day out for the whole of your career.

Under UK law, the presumption is that all adults have capacity to give legally valid consent to medical treatment. If, as the treating physician, you do not believe this to be the case, the onus is on you to justify this decision. The way in which capacity can be assessed is outlined in the case above.

Having separated patients into those with and those without capacity, the following are some short notes on consent in these groups.

Adults with capacity

- As a general rule, consent to treatment must be obtained from all adults with capacity.

- The process of gaining consent from a patient should ideally be undertaken by the person who is going to perform the procedure (they carry legal responsibility if the validity of consent is challenged). Failing this, the person obtaining consent should have a good understanding of the procedure.

- The patient must be aware that they are totally free to agree to, or refuse, the proposed treatment and that this consent can be withdrawn at any time.

- As explained above, (please refer to page 123) there are different measurements of the amount of information you should provide to a patient. However, in practice you should inform the patient of all significant, life-threatening and commonly occurring risks.

- You must also ensure that patients understand any medical terms used in the consenting process; where these are on the consent form, the accompanying explanation should also be recorded.

- The patient should be aware of what it is hoped will be achieved by undertaking the procedure, and any alternative treatment options. Again, if using a written consent form, this should be recorded.

- As explained above, there is no legal difference between valid written and valid oral consent. However the GMC recommends you should obtain written consent in cases where (see footnote [2] page 127):

    a. The treatment or procedure is complex, or involves significant risks and/or side-effects.

    b. Providing clinical care is not the primary purpose of the investigation or examination.

    c. There may be significant consequences for the patient's employment, social or personal life.

    d. The treatment is part of a research programme.

 Standard consent forms are now used in most NHS hospitals (and can be viewed at www.dh.gov.uk).

Consent in Adults

- Where consent is obtained a significant time in advance of a procedure, it should be reconfirmed before the procedure takes place. If in doubt as to whether a time interval is significant reconfirm.

- Except in cases of emergency, you should ensure that patients have reasonable time to contemplate and make a decision; they should be aware of the contents of the consent form in advance of the treatment, not as they are being wheeled down to theatre! Otherwise, consent may not be valid.

- Only in cases of emergency can a clinician go beyond what is authorised on the consent form. In this situation he/she should act in the patient's best interests, as with patients without capacity. Any advance refusals of treatment must be respected.

Adults without capacity

- Where an adult is judged not to have capacity to consent to treatment, the treating clinician must decide what is best for the patient, what is in their best interests.

- Detail on the factors you should consider in assessing best interests are given above but, broadly speaking, you must decide if the patient would want the treatment (were they able to decide for themselves), given what you know about the patient's views and beliefs. You also must also be sure that the treatment is clinically necessary.

- Any valid advance refusal of treatment made when the patient had capacity must be abided by. Advance requests for treatment should be considered as a formal record of the patient's prior views on certain treatments, but you are not under an obligation to provide these treatments where you consider it not in the patient's best interests.

- You should certainly talk to those close to the patient, their friends and family. You may also want to talk to the patient's GP and other health care professionals.

- Currently no one can give consent of behalf of another adult (except in Scotland where a legal proxy may be appointed). However, this will change; see the notes on the Mental Capacity Act below.

- Where a consensus cannot be reached as to what is in the patient's best interests, legal advice should be sought as to whether a court order is necessary.

- Donation of regenerative tissue such as bone marrow and sterilisation for contraceptive purposes must always receive prior High Court approval.

- Involving patients without capacity in research programmes is a legal hornets' nest, and you must seek specialist advice.

- If a patient is likely to regain capacity, you can only proceed with an investigation/treatment if you are satisfied that you cannot wait until they do so. Even then you should restrict treatment to that necessary to keep the patient alive.

- The decision-making process should be documented in the patient's notes. Consent Form 4 (a Department of Health document) can be used to record the important steps where an ordinary consent form would usually be necessary (in a situation where the patient has capacity).

Consent in Adults

Special consent issues

Mental Capacity Act 2005

This Act received royal assent in 2005, and is likely to come into force in 2007. It will have great impact on consent in adults lacking capacity. The Act:

- Defines what is meant by 'persons who lack capacity'.

- Gives clear guidelines as to how best interests should be assessed.

- Sets out who has legal liability for care/treatment carried out in a person without capacity.

- Provides legal means to appoint substitute decision-makers (deputies), where a person lacks capacity.

- Gives rules concerning advance directives and research involving those lacking capacity.

- Establishes a new Court of Protection, which, among other functions, will appoint deputies.

Research

Particular ethical problems arise in the research setting, many of which concern the consenting process for patients involved. Some of these issues include:

- Whether there is any therapeutic benefit to the patient (or whether they believe there is one when there might not be).

- The use of a placebo. (Is it ever acceptable for patients to believe they are having a treatment when they are not?)

- Confidentiality (in participation, and in relation to collected data).

- Risks to patients. (What level of risk is acceptable?)

• The possibility of coercing vulnerable patients into participation.

Of course the justification for all of these problems is that research is in the interests, or for the greater good, of society as a whole. The process of consenting patients aims to go some way in dealing with some of the ethical concerns; that, as autonomous beings, if the patients are fully informed as to what is involved and its risks, their agreement to voluntarily participate might, it is argued, allay some of these worries. They should be allowed to take risks.

In the UK all research is subject to Ethics Committee approval, where issues such as those outlined above are considered in detail for each proposal, before allowing the study to commence.

 This is well covered on the COREC (Central Office for Research Ethics Committees) website (www.corec.org.uk).

Teaching
Long gone are the days when merely being an inpatient in a teaching hospital indicated your consent to be involved with student teaching. The BMA gives the following brief advice (www.bma.org.uk):

Trusts must ensure that patients in teaching environments are aware of the possible presence of medical students in consultations or teaching sessions. Students must not examine patients, take histories, or undertake any procedure without the prior informed consent of the patient. Consent should be sought by the supervising member of the clinical team. Students should retain the right to refuse to commence or continue an examination, history or procedure, without fear of harassment, if it is not clear that informed consent has been obtained.

Consent in Adults

Mental illness

Patients suffering from a mental illness can be treated without their consent using two different legal means, common law and the Mental Health Act.

Common law – if a patient with mental illness lacks capacity, they may be treated in their best interests without their consent (see above), as with any other incompetent patient. However, the diagnosis of a mental illness does not necessarily confer lack of capacity; this should be assessed as set out previously. (Can they understand and retain the information? Do they believe it? Can they weigh it up?)

The Mental Health Act – this Act can be used to assess and treat those with, or suspected of having, a mental illness **for that mental illness**. There is no provision under this Act for treating patients for other medical and surgical complaints, or for detaining them against their will, except for the assessment and treatment of mental illness. Different sections of the Act have different powers, and a summary of some of these is shown below:

- **Section 2** – May be used to detain a patient suspected of mental illness for inpatient psychiatric assessment for up to 28 days, if the patient is a risk to themselves/others or the illness is of sufficient severity. Applied for by an approved social worker and nearest relative, and confirmed by two doctors.

- **Section 3** – Provides means to detain patients with known psychiatric disorders for up to 6 months initially, then for up to a year after review, for assessment and treatment of mental disorders. Applied for by an approved social worker and nearest relative, confirmed by two doctors.

- **Section 4** – Gives one doctor the power to urgently detain a patient for up to 72 hours if they absolutely cannot wait for a second doctor to be called (it would be dangerous) in order to use section 2. Applied for by an approved social worker or nearest relative, confirmed by one doctor (often the GP).

- **Section 5(2)** – The only one you are likely to see used in a general hospital. Can be used by the patient's consultant or named junior (except pre-registration house officer/foundation year 1 doctor) to detain inpatients for up to 72 hours if they are suffering from a mental disorder and are a danger to themselves and others (includes acute confusional state).

- **Section 135** – Can be used by the police to remove someone with known/suspected illness from their home (or other private place) to a place of safety for up to 72 hours. Warrant issued by a magistrate, at the request of an approved social worker.

- **Section 136** – Allows the police to remove someone known/suspected to have a mental illness from a public place to a place of safety for up to 72 hours.

Consent for testing for human immunodeficiency virus (HIV)

The Department of Health has recommended that informed consent should be obtained before testing for HIV infection. This should entail pre-test discussion, which in summary should include:[3]

1. **Making sure the patient understands what HIV is, how it is transmitted, and how to reduce the risk of this.**

2. **Obtaining information on any activities the patient has been involved in that might leave them at increased risk of having been infected with HIV, and explaining why a test is needed.**

[3]Department of Health *Guidelines for pre-test discussion on HIV*. 1996. (available at www.dh.gov.uk. Last accessed March 2006)

3. Explaining the benefits and disadvantages of knowing the HIV test result (whether positive or negative) and the implications of this for the patient, their family and acquaintances.

4. Ensuring the patient understands what the test involves and how they will receive the result.

5. Obtaining informed consent (if a decision has been made to go ahead with the test) and recording this in the patient's clinical record.

 For full details of the Department of Health Guidelines see www.dh.gov.uk

SCENARIO 7:
ORGAN DONATION

ANSWERS

SCENARIO 7: ORGAN DONATION

Dave is a 25-year-old engineer who was diagnosed with polycystic kidney disease. He progressed to end-stage renal failure (ESRF), and received a transplant. However, he did not attend the clinic or take his anti-rejection drugs regularly and his transplant failed. Suniti is a 32-year-old mother of three children, who also has ESRF as the result of diabetes. They are both receiving dialysis three times a week at their local hospital, and are on the transplant list.

Q List 4 criteria that may be used to prioritise patients waiting for transplant. **4 marks**

1. **The likelihood of the transplant being successful, eg donor and recipient tissue type (racial minorities are less likely to receive a transplant because they are less likely to have exact HLA matching).**

2. **The urgency of the recipient's condition.**

3. **The likely improvements to the recipient's quality of life.**

4. **The likely duration of benefit, eg the duration of benefit is likely to be greater in a child than in an elderly person.**

5. **Length of time on the waiting list.**

Organ Donation

QUESTIONS
PAGES 37–42

139

🛈 For patients on the kidney transplant waiting list, organ allocation is based on the best tissue match. In situations where two people have an equal match a points system is used, which looks at impartial factors such as time on the waiting list, age difference from donor, and 'matchability'.

🛈 Non-judgemental factors such as likelihood of transplant success are particularly useful where the patient's lifestyle may have an impact on a treatment decision. For example, ongoing abuse of alcohol may adversely affect the outcome of liver transplantation and the transplant could be denied legitimately on the grounds of futility.

Q Give 2 arguments for and 2 arguments against prioritisation on the basis of self-inflicted illness. **4 marks**

For:

1. **Intuitively, it is unfair that those that did not cause their illness wait behind those who did.**

2. **It sets a good example to society to look after one's health.**

3. **That, subversively, it may already occur; better to recognise this and be open about it.**

4. **It may be politically popular.**

Against:

1. **It can be very difficult to decide if illness is self-inflicted. (How many cigarettes do you have to have smoked for it to be your fault you have lung cancer?)**

2. **You are dealing with matters of life and death and in putting someone lower on the transplant list you may be issuing a 'death sentence'.**

Organ Donation

3. **Those who take good care of their health already benefit (they have better health than someone in the same position who doesn't).**

4. **Patients should be treated without judging them.**

🜂 Due to limited resources (and seemingly unlimited demands) the NHS continually has to make difficult decisions on allocating resources, whether it is money, time, equipment, staff or organs. Such decisions involve a range of financial, political and ethical considerations (see Teaching notes).

Dave receives his second organ transplant, but Suniti is still waiting. She has heard it is more difficult for people of Asian origin to find a compatible donor.

Q What are the disadvantages of the current 'organ donation' system?   *4 marks*

1. **Most people do not make their views known about organ donation.**

2. **Many people do not know how to register their wishes.**

3. **Donors may not be carrying their donor card at time of death.**

4. **When the patient's wishes are unknown it involves asking relatives at a very difficult and emotional time for permission to use their loved one's organs: 30% refuse such a request, though they often say later that they wish they hadn't.**

5. **The current system is unable to meet the increasing demands for organ transplantation.**

Organ Donation

🛈 The current organ donation system is an 'opt-in' system in that people who wish to donate need to either register their wishes on the NHS organ donor register and/or carry an organ donor card. Unfortunately, while approximately 90% of the population would be willing to donate, only 20% carry a donor card or are on the donor register.

🛈 Nearly 8000 people in the UK are on the transplant waiting list (this underestimates the need as people are only placed on the waiting list if they are considered to have a reasonable chance of receiving an organ). Furthermore, the waiting list continues to grow (it has increased by approximately 30% over the last 10 years) and every year several hundred patients die while on the list.

 For further details on becoming a donor visit www.uktransplant.org.uk.

Q What are the advantages of presumed consent?   *4 marks*

The advantages of presumed consent, where the patient is presumed to consent to organ donation unless they have registered their objections, include:

1. **The majority of people would like to donate (see above).**

2. **May prompt more discussion on organ donation amongst families.**

3. **Rather than requiring the majority who would like to donate to carry a donor card or put their name on the organ donor register, presumed consent requires the minority who don't want to donate to register their objection.**

4. **It is more cost-effective to maintain a register of the minority who do not want to donate rather than the majority who are willing to be donors.**

5. **Relieves relatives of having to make difficult decisions about donation during a difficult and emotional time.**

 The BMA supports a 'soft' system of presumed consent which means relatives' views are still taken into account. However, instead of being asked to consent to donation, they would be informed that the relative had not opted out of donation and, unless they object, donation would proceed.

> The BMA's position paper is available at their website (www.bma.org.uk)

You hear that Suniti has been talking to other patients on the dialysis unit and that her husband is thinking of taking her to India to 'buy her a new kidney'.

Q Give 2 arguments for and 2 arguments against allowing kidney sales. **4 marks**

For:

1. **It already exists, albeit illegally; legalising kidney sales will make the process more transparent, less likely to be abused and potentially available to all who require a transplant.**

2. **It will help reduce the NHS transplant waiting list.**

3. **It increases the autonomy of the donor: the donor may be anxious to sell their kidney in order to increase their own (and family's) quality of life.**

4. **It increases the autonomy of the recipient: it increases their likelihood of receiving a new kidney.**

Against:

1. **It discriminates against the poor, who are both unable to afford a transplant and coerced to donate their kidney due to money concerns.**

Organ Donation

2. **It will undermine confidence in the medical profession because of the association of doctors with a money-making practice.**

3. **It may lead to the slippery slope of selling vital organs such as hearts.**

The Human Organs Transplant Act 1989 was introduced in direct response to the 'kidneys for sale' scandal that exposed an international trade in human organs. Under this Act making or receiving payments (except expenses) for the supply of any organ is illegal. This applies both to live and dead donors. The legislation also applies to restrictions on live donation of organs. Those who are closely related must provide evidence of the relationship before proceeding. For unrelated donors (including long-term partners), the donation may not proceed until approval has been received from the Unrelated Live Transplant Regulatory Authority (ULTRA).

Total: **20 marks**

SCENARIO 7: ORGAN DONATION

 TEACHING NOTES

Resource allocation and organ transplantation

Health care resources

In the UK there are two major factors that restrict health care resources. The first of these are political/economic – how much capital the government is willing to invest in our health care system. The National Health Service must compete with other areas demanding funding, for example defence and education. Secondly, there are areas of provision affected by factors that no amount of money can rectify, eg organs for transplantation.

Monetary resource allocation decisions are then usually considered under two headings:

- **Macroallocation** – decisions made at government/assembly level (eg between financing education or health).

- **Microallocation** – decisions made at local level (eg within a hospital), for example, which department to give new equipment to.

So how should we divide up resources? In the case above, should Dave receive lower prioritisation because he may have caused his previous transplant to fail? Should Suniti be pushed up the list as she has three children to care for?

Other arguments might include:

- Prioritising cheaper treatments that benefit many rather than expensive treatments that benefit few.

- Prioritising the treatment of young people (with more years of life to benefit) over that of the old.

- Prioritising working people (who contribute taxes) over those that don't.

- Funding treatments that save lives over those that just improve it.

- Politics, refusing to treat certain groups for free, eg asylum seekers.

- Giving priority to treatments that have a high success rate over those that do not.

Do you think any of the arguments above are valid?

In the main, medical practitioners are deeply uncomfortable with having to make resource decisions on anything other than a clinical basis (eg how likely a treatment is to work). Doctors have a duty to their individual patients, but government and health care managers have to be concerned with the wider picture; they have a duty to the population as a whole – they must ensure **equity.**

The National Institute for Health and Clinical Excellence (NICE)

This organisation was established in April 2005 after NICE acquired roles of the Health Development Agency. They list their work under three areas (see www.nice.org.uk):

- Technology appraisals – guidance on the use of new and existing medicines and treatments within the NHS in England and Wales.

- Clinical guidelines – guidance on the appropriate treatment and care of people with specific diseases and conditions.

- Interventional procedures – guidance on whether interventional procedures used for diagnosis or treatment are safe enough and work well enough for routine use.

The role of NICE in evaluating new technologies has affected resource allocation in particular. One of the ambitions in establishing NICE was to try to eliminate inequalities in access to effective health care nationwide, the so-called 'postcode lottery'. In its technology assessments NICE brings together the issues of clinical efficacy and cost effectiveness before making recommendations, which then fall into three categories:

1. Recommended for use throughout the NHS (either generally or for specific patient groups/clinical indications).

2. Recommended for use in clinical trials only.

3. Not recommended for use in the NHS (due to lack of evidence for clinical/cost-effectiveness).

There have been two consequences of this that have hit the headlines:

1. Funding authorities have been reluctant in some cases to fund new treatments without NICE guidance. For example, the Department of Health said of this in relation to bortezomib (Velcade®), a drug used in multiple myeloma, 'It is unacceptable for primary care trusts and other health bodies to use a lack of NICE guidance as an excuse for refusing to consider evidence in reaching decisions on whether to make new treatments available on the NHS.' (see www.parliament.the-stationery-office.co.uk)

Organ Donation

2. Some treatments already in use have been deemed to lack clinical evidence or not be cost-effective for certain uses. For example, recommendations that the NHS should only fund the use of Alzheimer's drugs donepezil, rivastigmine and galantamine in circumstances more limited than previously caused great upset among those representing this patient group.

Read more about NICE at
www.nice.org.uk

QALYs

One of the tools used by NICE and other bodies in assessing the cost-effectiveness of treatments and other health care interventions, QALY stands for **q**uality-**a**djusted **l**ife **y**ear. The principle is fairly simple. It gives a numerical value to 1 year of life, adjusted according to the quality of that year of life. So 1 year of perfect health would be given a score of 1.0, and in less good health a score, for example, of 0.7. They provide a standardised measure that can be used to compare different treatments/procedures.

Problems with QALYs:

1. Some treatments many consider valuable fare badly, eg palliative care.

2. It is difficult to assign a numerical value to quality of life; which is worse – being bed-bound or being in pain?

3. QALYs may be ageist – older people do not have as many years to live in which to benefit from an intervention and so will score poorly.

4. They may discriminate against those with disability, who can never be returned to full health, but may well benefit from an intervention for an acute illness.

Proponents of QALYs argue that many of the above are just a reflection of the rigorous nature of the QALY, that, for example, it is reasonable for the elderly to score worse, as treatments for young

Organ Donation

people really are more valuable. This is called the 'fair opportunity' principle: what is important is the opportunity you have for health averaged out over a whole lifetime, not just part of it. In other words, if you survive to 80 in good health you should forego resources in favour of someone younger who has not achieved maximal life expectancy and who has not had fair opportunity to benefit.

Organ transplantation

The problem of lack of resources is particularly difficult in relation to organ transplants.

Under the current system in the UK, after the death of a person who may be suitable for organ donation, the relatives are approached and asked to give their consent for organ harvest. This can be fraught with problems. Often the relatives have little idea as to what their loved one would have wanted.

The legal position

Organ transplantation is overseen in the UK by the UK Transplant Support Service Authority (UKTSSA).

There are two pieces of legislation that govern organ transplantation:

- The Human Tissue Act 1961

- The Human Organ Transplants Act 1989

These are both shortly to be superseded by Human Tissue Act 2004, due to come into force in 2006.

The Human Tissue Act seeks 'to make provision with respect to the use of parts of bodies of deceased persons for therapeutic purposes and purposes of medical education and research and with respect to the circumstances in which post-mortem examination may be carried out; and to permit cremation of bodies removed for anatomical examination.[1]

[1]The Human Tissue Act 1961, cited at www.uktransplant.org.uk

Organ Donation

Under section 1(1) of this Act a person can, in the presence of two witnesses, in writing at any time or orally during their last illness, request that all or any specified part of their body can be used for organ transplant (or for any other medical research or teaching purpose).

Section 2 gives permission to the hospital in possession of the body after death to remove organs for transplantation (unless permission has been withdrawn).

Legally, organs can be harvested for transplant from someone known to have given consent before death without the permission of their relatives. In reality, however, this is unlikely to happen.

The Human Organ Transplants Act bans payment for organs. Sections 2(1) and 2(2) provide legal means for organ transplantation between living close relations. Section 2(3) of the Act and the Human Organ Transplants (Unrelated Persons) Regulations 1989 give permission for transplants between unrelated people as long as this has been approved by ULTRA (the Unrelated Live Transplant Regulatory Authority). For ULTRA to agree to an unrelated transplant, they must be satisfied that there has been no payment or coercion involved.

Presumed consent

The BMA supports a system of presumed consent, whereby all individuals would be presumed to have given consent for their organs to be used for transplant, unless they have given express refusal. The arguments for and against this are as follows:

For:

1. It may increase the numbers of organs available for transplant.

2. Research has shown the majority of the UK population would be happy to be organ donors after their death.

3. It costs less to record those who object, compared with recording those who don't.

4. It would relieve grieving families of the burden of having to decide.

Against:

1. Removing organs from a person whose relatives do not want this would cause extreme distress.

2. It is very unusual for relatives to refuse consent in cases where it is known that the deceased wished to be a donor.

3. Failure to withdraw consent may reflect lack of understanding or information rather than agreement with the process.

4. The policy of requiring families to give consent promotes trust and confidence in UK transplant services.

 You can read opposing sides of the debate at www.uktransplant.org.uk (against) and www.bma.org.uk (for)

Organ Donation

SCENARIO 8: CONFIDENTIALITY

ANSWERS

SCENARIO 8: CONFIDENTIALITY

During his teenage years Stephen contracted hepatitis C while experimenting with intravenous drugs. He hasn't touched drugs for over 10 years now and is happily married, with a responsible job. At one of his regular outpatient appointments his gastroenterologist offers him the chance to participate in a clinical trial to help clear his virus.

Q In seeking Stephen's consent, what information about the trial needs to be provided?   *5 marks*

1. **Purpose of the research.**

2. **What the trial involves.**

3. **Probability of allocation to the treatment or placebo (or standard treatment) groups.**

4. **Information about benefits and risks.**

5. **Advice that they can withdraw at any time during the research (for any reason) without harming their relationship with their doctor.**

6. **Available expenses, including compensation in the event of harm occurring (though patients must participate voluntarily, ie they cannot be bribed).**

7. **How personal information will be collected, stored, shared and published.**

Confidentiality

QUESTIONS
PAGES 43–48

8. Confirmation that the research has been approved by a research ethics committee (REC): see Teaching notes.

🟊 Seeking consent is fundamental to research. Consent is only legally valid if the patient is competent to give consent, has been properly informed and has agreed to participate voluntarily, without coercion. The generic issues around seeking consent, including assessing capacity, are discussed in greater detail in Scenario 6, Consent in adults. Seeking consent in children and incapacitated adults for research purposes is discussed in the Teaching notes for this scenario.

Stephen is keen to participate in the trial but is concerned that as a result his employers may discover he is hepatitis C positive.

Q Why is confidentiality important?   *2 marks*

1. Respects patient autonomy.

2. Maximises patient–doctor trust.

🟊 Confidentiality is important for two reasons: firstly, because it respects patient autonomy, ie the right to have control over their own life, and secondly because confidentiality is central to trust between doctors and patients.

🟊 Confidentiality is enshrined in the GMC's guidance – *Duties of a Doctor*. Two of these duties are:
  • respect patient's dignity and privacy
  • respect and protect confidential information

Q How do you protect patient confidentiality?   *4 marks*

1. Avoid disclosing information unless it is necessary.

2. Anonymise data where unidentifiable data will serve the purpose.

3. Keep any disclosures to the bare minimum.

4. Ensure colleagues also maintain confidentiality: it's important that patients are aware that personal information may be shared within the health care team.

5. Always seek patient's consent before disclosing.

6. Always ensure patient information is adequately protected, eg do not leave files around: this is governed by the Data Protection Act 1998.

7. Take reasonable steps to ensure any consultations are private and cannot be overheard (though this is very hard to achieve with bedside consultations).

🐠 It is notable that in the Netherlands the low rates of teenage pregnancies has in part been attributed to assurances regarding patient–doctor confidentiality when prescribing contraceptives.

Q Under what situations may breach of patient confidence be justifiable? **5 marks**

1. Disclosures to statutory bodies, eg communicable diseases, termination of pregnancy, births and deaths.

2. Under court orders.

3. Sharing information with other members of the health care team in the interests of the patient.

4. In the public interest, eg in the prevention, or investigation of a serious crime; or where a third party is at significant risk (eg a partner of an HIV-positive person).

5. In the patient's interest, eg sexual abuse, neglect.

6. When a patient who is not medically fit to drive continues to do so: you need to inform the Driving and Vehicle Licensing Agency (DVLA) medical officer.

Confidentiality

157

🛈 Doctors are legally obliged to maintain patient confidentiality, though this obligation is not absolute and there are situations in which doctors **must** breach confidentiality (1 and 2 above) and situations which **allow** breach of confidentiality (3–6 above).

🛈 You should, where possible, inform patients of such disclosures and try to obtain their consent, though ultimately under these situations consent is not required and disclosure may proceed even if consent is withheld. This principle has been supported in the courts.

🛈 A schizophrenic patient (W) detained in a secure mental hospital for the killing of five people applied for a transfer to a less secure hospital. The patient's solicitors approached a psychiatrist (Egdell) to prepare a report on the patient's mental health, ultimately hoping that such a report would support their application. When it became apparent that the report opposed the transfer they failed to make the report available. The psychiatrist, realising his report would not be taken into consideration, attempted to forward it onto the Home Secretary. The patient's solicitors sought to prevent this, though ultimately the courts supported this breach of confidentiality on the basis that it was in the public interest (*W* v *Egdell* 1989 1 All ER 835).

Stephen is satisfied by your reassurances of confidentiality and commences on the trial the following week.

Q What are your responsibilities as a researcher?   *4 marks*

When performing research, to ensure you always act in the patients' best interests, the following ethical principles should be followed:

Confidentiality

1. It is not ethical to repeat research already performed.

2. The research must be designed to achieve a desired, worthwhile goal (even if it subsequently fails to achieve that).

3. Foreseeable side-effects should be identified and where possible minimised.

4. You must ensure the research protocol has been approved by a research ethics committee (REC).

5. You must follow all aspects of the protocol: any significant changes must be agreed by the REC.

6. You must ensure that patients participate voluntarily, without coercion or under pressure.

7. Informed consent (where appropriate) should have been obtained: see first question above.

8. You must maintain complete and accurate records.

9. Ensure patient confidentiality is maintained (see above).

10. You must ensure that you are not influenced by payments or gifts and that any fraud or misconduct is reported to the appropriate body.

11. Publish the results where possible, including adverse or negative findings.

12. Any results (either positive or negative) which warrant stopping the trial early on ethical grounds should be reported as soon as possible.

Total: **20 marks**

These ethical principles governing medical research are enshrined in the *World Medical Association Declaration of Helsinki: ethical principles for medical research involving human subjects* (available at www.cirp.org)

Confidentiality

SCENARIO 8: CONFIDENTIALITY

TEACHING NOTES

Good medical practice depends on establishing good patient–doctor trust. Confidentiality is central to this trust. Without assurances about confidentiality, patients may be reluctant to provide information or allow intimate examinations that are necessary for providing good care. To protect patient confidentiality the GMC[1] recommend that when asked to provide information about a patient you should:

• Keep any disclosures to the bare minimum.

• Anonymise data where unidentifiable data will serve the purpose.

• Seek the patient's consent to disclosure of information.

Breaches of confidence can have serious repercussions on the doctor–patient relationship. If the patient discovers the breach, he or she may lose trust in that doctor or doctors in general, resulting in their receiving less effective health care. Similarly, if the general public is left with the impression that doctors do not maintain confidentiality this could have a general negative effect on the delivery of health care.

Confidentiality

[1]General Medical Council (GMC) *Confidentiality: protecting and providing information* (available at www.gmc-uk.org Last accessed March 2006)

Express consent is needed for disclosure for the purposes of research, administration (eg insurance reports) and audit (if data cannot be anonymised). When seeking such consent you must ensure that patients are aware what information is being disclosed, the purpose of the disclosure and the likely consequences. If the patient withholds consent or consent cannot be obtained, you can only disclose if required by law or if disclosure is in the public interest.

There are numerous situations in which doctors **must not** breach confidentiality. These include casual breaches (eg gossiping, failure to anonymise data), preventing **minor** harm to others, or in the prevention, detection or processing of a **minor** crime. However, while doctors are legally obliged to maintain patient confidentiality, this obligation is not absolute and there are situations in which doctors **must** breach confidentiality (to specific authorities only) and situations which **allow** breach of confidentiality (these breaches are at the doctor's discretion and should ideally be made in consultation with colleagues).

Examples where doctors **must** breach confidentiality:

- Notifiable diseases: under the Notifiable Diseases Act 1984.

- Termination of pregnancy: under the Abortion Act 1967.

- Births and deaths: under the Births and Deaths Registration Act 1953.

- Under court orders.

Examples where doctors are **allowed** to breach confidentiality:

- Sharing information with other members of the health care team in the interests of the patient.

- In the public interest, eg in the prevention, detection or prosecution process of a **serious** crime, or when a third party is at significant risk (eg a partner of an HIV-positive person).

Confidentiality

- In the patient's interest, eg sexual abuse, neglect.

- When a patient who is not medically fit to drive continues to do so: you need to inform the DVLA medical officer.

You should, where possible, inform patients of such disclosures and try to obtain their consent, though ultimately under these situations consent is not required and disclosure may proceed even if consent is withheld. Clearly there will be some situations where it is not practicable to obtain consent, eg from a dangerous patient, or when there is insufficient time to contact the patient (eg in reporting a communicable disease).

 There are extensive resources about NHS confidentiality and the Caldicott principles at the Department of Health website (www.dh.gov.uk).

Research

Medical research is fundamental to medical practice. When performing research, to ensure you always act in the patients' best interests the following ethical principles should be followed:[2]

- It is not ethical to repeat research already performed.

- The research must be designed to achieve a desired, worthwhile goal (even if it subsequently fails to achieve that).

- Foreseeable side-effects should have been identified and where possible minimised.

- You must ensure the research protocol has been approved by a research committee.

- You must follow all aspects of the protocol: any significant changes must be agreed by the research committee.

[2]World Medical Association Declaration of Helsinki: ethical principles for medical research involving human subjects www.cirp.org Last accessed February 2006

Confidentiality

- You must ensure that patients participate voluntarily, without coercion or under pressure.

- Informed consent (where appropriate) should be obtained.

- You must maintain complete and accurate records.

- Ensure patient confidentiality is maintained.

- You must ensure that you are not influenced by payments or gifts and that any fraud or misconduct is reported to the appropriate body.

- Publish the results where possible, including adverse or negative findings.

- Any results (either positive or negative) which warrant stopping the trial early on ethical grounds should be reported as soon as possible.

Ensuring that valid informed consent has been obtained respects patient autonomy. When seeking informed consent the following information needs to be provided:

- Purpose of the research.

- What the trial involves.

- Probability of allocation to the treatment or placebo (or standard treatment) groups.

- Information about benefits and risks.

- Advice that they can withdraw at any time during the research (for any reason) without harming their relationship with their doctor.

- Available expenses, including compensation in the event of harm occurring (though patients must participate voluntarily, ie they cannot be bribed).

Confidentiality

- How personal information will be collected, stored, shared and published.

- Confirmation that the research has been approved by an ethics committee.

Research ethics committees (RECs) are either local (eg hospital-based) or multicentre (to review research carried out at various centres). Such committees typically contain a scientist, a statistician, a lawyer, an ethicist, at least one health professional and a lay person. Research which has not been approved by an REC is unlikely to be accepted for publication.

In clinical trials (the gold standard of medical research) it is only ethical to use a placebo (as opposed to standard treatment) if no effective treatment already exists. Those in the non-treatment group may appear to be disadvantaged, although: (1) they may be spared unforeseen side-effects; (2) if the trial reveals the treatment has a negative effect they will benefit; and (3) if the ongoing trial demonstrates a positive benefit of the treatment under question the trial can be stopped early so that **all** participants subsequently receive the best treatment.

Medical research can broadly be classified into:

- Therapeutic research, ie research that benefits the patient directly (performed in patients with the condition in question).

- Non-therapeutic research, ie research that benefits others (typically performed in healthy consenting adults).

When performing **therapeutic** research in children, incapacitated adults or competent but vulnerable adults (eg frail elderly people, those with a terminal illness) you need to ensure:

- That the research cannot be carried out in competent healthy adults.

Confidentiality

- That the research will advantage similar individuals, eg if performed in children, it will be of potential benefit to children.

- That the research is in the patient's best interest.

- Where possible, that the patient has given informed consent. For example, in some illnesses (eg Alzheimer's disease) mental capacity fluctuates, allowing consent to be obtained; children may have sufficient understanding to consent to some forms of research (see Scenario 2, Consent in minors).

- That informed consent has been obtained from those with parental responsibility (in the case of children).

It is much harder to justify non-therapeutic research in these cohorts (as opposed to healthy, consenting adults) though it may be justified if there is minimal risk, if it does not involve any suffering, if the participant does not object (either physically or verbally), if consent has been given if possible, and if approval has been given by an ethics committee. The legal issues surrounding this area are very complicated, and specialist advice is likely to be required when planning research in this group.

Fuller guidelines are available from the GMC General Medical Council (GMC). (*Research: the role and responsibilities of doctors.* (available at www.gmc-uk.org Last accessed February 2006)

Confidentiality

USEFUL WEBSITES

www.bailii.org
British and Irish Legal Information Institute

www.bbc.co.uk/religion

www.bma.org.uk
British Medical Association

www.cirp.org
Circumcision Information and Resources Pages

www.corec.org.uk
Central Office for Research Ethics Committees

www.dca.gov.uk
Department of Constitutional Affairs – Justice, Rights and Democracy

www.dh.gov.uk
Department of Health

www.dignityindying.org.uk
Dignity in dying (formerly www.ves.org.uk). Leading campaigning organisation promoting patient choice at the end of life

www.ethox.org.uk
The Ethox Centre is dedicated to improving patient care through raising ethical understanding and ethical standards

www.gmc-uk.org
General Medical Council

www.nice.org.uk
NHS National Institute for Health and Clinical Excellence

www.opsi.gov.uk/acts
Office of Public Sector Information – details of new Public Acts of Parliament

www.publications.parliament.uk
The United Kingdom Parliament World Wide Web Service

www.thelancet.com
The Lancet Journal

www.uktransplant.org.uk
NHS Blood and Transplant

www.worldlii.org
World Legal Information Institute

INDEX

in children over 16 69–70
in children under the age of 16 70–71
to disclosure 158, 160, 161, 162
forms 124, 129, 131
implied 124
legally valid 34, 122, 124
in minors 9–12, 61–71
for non-therapeutic interventions 63, 64
obtaining 121
presumed, for organ donation 41, 142, 150–151
reconfirming 130
for research 156,163
to the presence of medical students 133
time to consider 130
validity challenged 129
when not legally required 35, 125–126
written 124, 129
consultations, privacy 157
contraception
advantages of confidentiality 157
Gillick competence 70–71
court orders 65–66, 109, 115, 131, 157, 161
CPR, when to attempt or not 4–5, 55–56

data, anonymising 156, 160
Data Protection Act 1998 157
decision-making process, documented in patient's notes 131
Devi v West Midlands RHA 122
disclosures
in the public interest 161
statutory 157
distributive justice 78, 84
'do not resuscitate' (DNR) order 3, 4, 52
doctor
disagreement with consensus decision 110
duties 156
legal obligations 113, 158, 161
psychological harm 79
see also patient–doctor relationship
donation *see* organ donation
donor card 141, 142
double effect 17, 81–82
Down's syndrome
screening 21, 22, 91–92
serious handicap 95
Driving and Vehicle Licensing Agency (DVLA) 157, 162
driving while not medically fit 157, 162

emergency protection order 66
emergency treatment 125, 130
end-of-life decision making, guidance 112
EPICure study 101
equity, ensuring 146
ethics committee 133, 156
see also research ethics committee
ethnic minorities, difficulty of finding matched donors 40, 139, 141

European Convention on Human Rights 57
European Court of Human Rights 87, 88–89, 102
euthanasia 13–17, 73–89
active and passive 16, 76–77
arguments against 78–89
arguments in favour 83–84
definition 75–76
involuntary/voluntary/non-voluntary 77
legal/regulatory aspects 78, 79

family
cannot overrule valid agreement to treatment 36, 127
consent to organ donation 141, 142, 143, 149
disagreement with advance directives 4
disagreement with doctors 29, 56, 88, 109, 115, 124–125
disagreement with patient 4, 35
distress 108
knowledge of patient's wishes 109, 115, 116, 127
of patient without capacity for consent 126
views must be sought 115, 116, 131
Family Law Reform Act 1969 63, 69
father
legal rights in decision to terminate pregnancy 23, 97
parental responsibility 65, 66
fetal abnormalities, diagnosis 101, 102, 103
fetus
moral status 102–103
right to life 102
viability 101

Germany, abortion on request 98
gestational age, for legal termination of pregnancy 22, 95, 97, 100, 103
Gillick competence 63, 64–65, 70–71, 97
Gillick v West Norfolk and Wisbech Area Health Authority 70
Glass v the United Kingdom 88–89, 126
gradualist approach to termination of pregnancy 102–103

handicap, serious 95, 101
Human Fertilisation and Embryology Act 1990 95, 99
human immunodeficiency virus (HIV), consent for testing 135–136
Human Organ Transplants Act 1989 144, 149, 150
Human Rights Act 1998 55, 57–59, 87, 88, 102, 110, 112
Human Tissue Act 1961 149
Human Tissue Act 2004 149–150

illness, self-inflicted 40, 140–141
information